Praise for *Cultural Competence Now*

A practical guide for educators who seek to overcome their biases so that they can be effective in the classroom and a source of support to all of the students they serve. We all have bias, but we can also unlearn our biases if we have an open mind and heart. This book has several thoughtful suggestions on how educators can do so. For those who seek to grow so that they can become genuine allies to the students and the communities they serve, this book will be an invaluable resource.

—Pedro A. Noguera, PhD
Distinguished Professor of Education
Faculty Director, Center for the Transformation of Schools
UCLA Graduate School of Education & Information Studies

~ ~ ~

Vernita Mayfield has written a book that strikes just the right balance among personal stories, theoretical rationale, and practical advice for educators to operationalize equity. We can't wait any longer to ensure that every educator in America has the skills they need to dismantle systems of oppression and confront institutional racism in schools. Dr. Mayfield's book can be used by any educator in any setting to start that work and become truly culturally competent.

—Joshua P. Starr, EdD
Chief Executive Officer, PDK International

Cultural Competence
NOW

ASCD MEMBER BOOK

Many ASCD members received this book as
a member benefit upon its initial release.

Learn more at www.ascd.org/memberbooks

Cultural Competence
NOW

56 Exercises to Help Educators
Understand and Challenge
Bias, Racism, and **Privilege**

VERNITA MAYFIELD

Alexandria, Virginia USA

1703 N. Beauregard St. EAlexandria, VA 22311-1714 USA
Phone: 800-933-2723 or 703-578-9600 EFax: 703-575-5400
Website: www.ascd.org EE-mail: member@ascd.org
Author guidelines: www.ascd.org/write

Ranjit Sidhu, *Executive Director and CEO;* Stefani Roth, *Publisher;* Genny Ostertag, *Director, Content Acquisitions;* Julie Houtz, *Director, Book Editing & Production;* Liz Wegner, *Editor;* Judi Connelly, *Senior Art Director;* Masie Chong, *Graphic Designer;* Circle Graphics, *Typesetter;* Kelly Marshall, *Interim Manager, Production Services;* Shajuan Martin, *E-Publishing Specialist;* Tristan Coffelt, *Senior Production Specialist*

Copyright © 2020 ASCD. All rights reserved. It is illegal to reproduce copies of this work in print or electronic format (including reproductions displayed on a secure intranet or stored in a retrieval system or other electronic storage device from which copies can be made or displayed) without the prior written permission of the publisher. By purchasing only authorized electronic or print editions and not participating in or encouraging piracy of copyrighted materials, you support the rights of authors and publishers. Readers who wish to reproduce or republish excerpts of this work in print or electronic format may do so for a small fee by contacting the Copyright Clearance Center (CCC), 222 Rosewood Dr., Danvers, MA 01923, USA (phone: 978-750-8400; fax: 978-646-8600; web: www.copyright.com). To inquire about site licensing options or any other reuse, contact ASCD Permissions at www.ascd.org/permissions, or permissions@ascd.org. For a list of vendors authorized to license ASCD e-books to institutions, see www.ascd.org/epubs. Send translation inquiries to translations@ascd.org.

ASCD® and ASCD LEARN. TEACH. LEAD.® are registered trademarks of ASCD. All other trademarks contained in this book are the property of, and reserved by, their respective owners, and are used for editorial and informational purposes only. No such use should be construed to imply sponsorship or endorsement of the book by the respective owners.

All web links in this book are correct as of the publication date below but may have become inactive or otherwise modified since that time. If you notice a deactivated or changed link, please e-mail books@ascd.org with the words "Link Update" in the subject line. In your message, please specify the web link, the book title, and the page number on which the link appears.

PAPERBACK ISBN: 978-1-4166-2849-1 ASCD product #118043
PDF E-BOOK ISBN: 978-1-4166-2891-0; see Books in Print for other formats.

Quantity discounts are available: e-mail programteam@ascd.org or call 800-933-2723, ext. 5773, or 703-575-5773. For desk copies, go to www.ascd.org/deskcopy.

ASCD Member Book No. FY20-5 (Feb. 2020 P). ASCD Member Books mail to Premium (P), Select (S), and Institutional Plus (I∗) members on this schedule: Jan, PSI∗; Feb, P; Apr, PSI∗; May, P; Jul, PSI∗; Aug, P; Sep, PSI∗; Nov, PSI∗; Dec, P. For current details on membership, see www.ascd.org/membership.

Library of Congress Cataloging-in-Publication Data

Names: Mayfield, Vernita, author.
Title: Cultural competence now : 56 exercises to help educators understand and challenge bias, racism, and privilege / Vernita Mayfield.
Description: Alexandria, Virginia : ASCD, [2020] | Includes bibliographical references and index.
Identifiers: LCCN 2019036091 (print) | LCCN 2019036092 (ebook) | ISBN 9781416628491 (paperback) | ISBN 9781416628910 (pdf)
Subjects: LCSH: Multicultural education—United States. | Cultural competence—United States. | Educational equalization--United States.
Classification: LCC LC1099.38 .M39 2020 (print) | LCC LC1099.38 (ebook) | DDC 370.117—dc23
LC record available at https://lccn.loc.gov/2019036091
LC ebook record available at https://lccn.loc.gov/2019036092

For Dr. Kamalee Williams.
Gleefully walking in your footsteps
from the moment I took my first steps.

Cultural
Competence
NOW

Introduction

Looking back on my 30 years in education, I can recall many microaggressions that were the result of lack of cultural competency and ignorance of personal bias or privilege. All too often, educators were oblivious to the perpetuation of systemic and institutional racism in schools and would fail to act or advocate on behalf of people historically oppressed. The lack of cultural competency in schools has very real consequences. Consider the examples that follow.

Bias Influences Disciplinary Outcomes for Students

Some years ago, as I sat chatting casually with colleagues, the topic of race arose. One colleague whom I respect deeply shared her earliest recollection of noticing race. "I grew up in a small town that was home to a large male prison facility," she began. "I was told that bad colored men lived there. Even though the prison was surrounded by large impervious walls, my mother would nervously lock the car doors and floor the gas pedal when she drove past it. From those early experiences, I learned to fear colored men," she continued. "African American men seemed dark, scary, emotionally volatile people who could potentially erupt into violence at any moment."

My colleague sighed with resignation. "I think I still harbor that fear to this day," she said.

My other colleagues seemed scarcely fazed. The speaker was a reputable school administrator of a large suburban school that struggled with disproportionate disciplinary outcomes for students of color.

Racism Limits Opportunity

I was attending a school-based leadership team meeting one evening when the conversation turned to planning an 8th grade culminating event. "What about a trip to Europe?" I offered. "My son's school plans one every year. We've got the whole year to raise funds. I'll bet the students would be highly motivated!"

One teacher's face twisted in horror. "What? These kids don't know anything about traveling to Europe!" she quipped. "*Maybe* a trip to Mexico, but they go there all the time anyway." Her comment brought nodding heads and chuckles from her colleagues—including the principal.

Privilege Labels and Oppresses Some While Providing for Others to Move Freely in Educational Spaces

I brought my 12-year-old son to school with me one day when our spring break schedules failed to align. The counselor designed a special class schedule for him and promised to introduce him to each of his teachers for the day. "It's only for a day," I assured him. "Come to my office later on, and we'll go out for lunch." He grinned up at me, his dark eyes and thick, kinky hair a mirrored reflection of my own. OK, so maybe he wasn't that excited about spending one of his vacation days in a school, but at that age, a Taco Bell lunch was all the bait I needed. "Now, go make some new friends!" I said, kissing him on the forehead before the counselor whisked him away.

That afternoon, as I made my rounds on the campus, a 6th grade teacher approached me. "Who's the new kid?" he queried. "What do you mean?" I answered, maybe a little too quickly. I thought my question fair, however, because new students enrolled all the time, usually without question. "Have you seen him?" he probed suspiciously. "Well, yes," I responded, trying not to be defensive, "What about him?" "He just looks like trouble," the teacher said, shaking his head. "I told Henry [a fellow teacher], we're going to have to keep a close eye on him because he looks like he comes from a rough part of town. Yep, I think he is nothing but trouble."

Racism Perpetuates Stereotypes and Limits Opportunity and Voice for People of Color

"I need you to write a white paper on the statewide approach to school turn-around," my colleague stated loudly to me. We were talking on speakerphone to a colleague working remotely from home, and the connection was poor. My colleague was without access to his regular office, so the meeting had to be conducted in the lunchroom, where another meeting was in progress in a nearby glassed room. He continued, "I need to present a white paper at a national meeting next week."

I was astounded and yet, not entirely. This wouldn't be the first time he had asked me to do his work while he took full credit at meetings that I was disallowed from attending. "Since I am writing the paper, why don't I present it?" I pushed back. "I'm the one who can best speak to my work and my words. I'm the one who could best answer questions regarding the report if they arise."

"No," he said shaking his head. "You're not going to this meeting. Walk me through the report ahead of time so I can answer all questions. Just write the report." I persisted this time. "As a researcher, I am accustomed to getting credit for my work, and why the heck shouldn't I?" He was visibly taken aback, not used to being confronted.

What happened next was far more alarming. A fellow education executive scurried to our table, looking about nervously. "I was asked to come out here and investigate what was going on," he whispered, red-faced and clearly flustered. Confused, we waited in silence. "Someone in the meeting next door reported a verbal fight between you two. They thought you [and he was looking expressly at me here] looked especially angry, and they were afraid what might happen next."

"Oh great," I moaned. "The default pejorative stance of any Black woman who speaks assertively or authoritatively is 'angry.'" What else could it possibly be? (The sad truth is that people of color jump on that bandwagon just as quickly as anyone else. But that's a complexity of historical racial paradigms that deserves its own book.)

Lack of Cultural Competency Maintains Economic Inequality and Perpetuates the Cumulative Impact of Income Disparity in Families of Color

I glared at the district report in front of me. There it was in black and white—the list of administrators in the district, along with their current salaries. It was an ordinary report that the school board reviewed annually, but this was the first time I had laid eyes on it. And there it was. Every administrator in the district earned $20,000 to $30,000 more than I did, the first and only administrator of color in the district—even the preschool principal, who had a fraction of the student population of my secondary school!

My supervisor recognized my angst. "I guess you are wondering why your salary is so much lower. Well," she explained nervously, "all the other administrators came from affluent school districts where they were earning high salaries. We only offer a certain percentage higher than one's previous salary." She shrugged her shoulders as if helpless. "What could we do? We couldn't offer them less."

The Harsh Reality

If these were the only experiences I had with a lack of cultural competency or ignorance of socioeconomic inequities perpetuated in K–16 education systems, this book would scarcely be worth the effort. The truth is, I could write a book with *nothing but* examples of bias and inequity in educational systems, and it would be brimming with interesting and, at times, shocking stories. What would be the point though?

No, I wrote this book for all the generally well-meaning, hard-working educators going about their day-to-day work, espousing beliefs of meritocracy through education and exercising what they perceive to be equality in practice, while sacrificing students and educators of color on the altar of implicit bias, racism, and cultural ignorance.

Too harsh? Hardly. The data are profoundly clear:

- Black, Hispanic, and Native American students are suspended and expelled in disproportionately greater numbers than their white peers, including preschoolers. This is fundamentally true in most states, school districts, and schools across the United States (Gregory, Skiba, & Noguera, 2010; Monroe, 2005; Townsend, 2000).
- Children of color are overrepresented in special education classes and have been for years (Boyd & Correa, 2005; Griner & Stewart, 2013).

- Students of color are less likely to be enrolled in advanced placement (AP) classes (Taliaferro & DeCuir-Gunby, 2008).
- The high school graduation rates for students of color are lower than those for whites and Asians: 72 percent for American Indians, 78 percent for Blacks, 80 percent for Hispanics, compared to 89 percent for whites and 91 percent for Asians in 2016–2017 (National Center for Education Statistics, 2019a).
- The vast majority of public school teachers identify as white, about 80 percent. Representation from teachers of color is significantly lower. Hispanic teachers make up almost 10 percent, Black teachers about 7 percent, multiracial teachers about 1 percent, and Asians or Pacific Islanders fewer than 1 percent in 2015–2016 (National Center for Education Statistics, 2019f).
- Educators of all races and ethnicities manifest negative assumptions and perceptions about people of color even before they begin work in schools (Amatea, Cholewa, & Mixon, 2012; Fasching-Varner, 2009; Gay & Kirkland, 2003; Middleton, 2002).
- Educators of color are not immune to unconscious bias in the workplace. Microaggressions and macroaggressions against people of color are perpetuated routinely by colleagues, parents, supervisors, and students, often unknowingly, though sometimes with full intent (Jay, 2009).

Having studied the abundance of empirical research on the intersection of culture, race, and inequity in schools and having spent 30 years in education, I decided to assess my choices concerning how I might respond. I could

1. Recite the dismal statistics on inequity in education to anyone who would listen.
2. Blame educational systems for their failure to meet the needs of all their constituents.
3. Ignore the prevailing facts on disparate outcomes for students of color, and hope for the best.

However, none of those choices reflect me or what I've fought for as an urban school educator. The only real choice for me was to contribute to the body of work that builds the cultural competency of educators, unpacks personal bias and privilege, and promotes antiracism and the value of being an ally for social justice.

About This Book

Cultural Competence Now is designed to respond to the urgent need to build the cultural competency of educators—for the sake of children, first of all, but also in the interest of supporting and retaining all educators in the workplace. After more than 50 years of gnawing on the data of differential outcomes for students of color, after more than 300 years of systems that ignore the implications of historical trauma and socioeconomic inequality on students and families of color, after watching too many educators throw in the towel of frustration, it's time we swallow the bitter pill of racial dialogues and begin the examination of deeply embedded bias, values, and beliefs about differences that have prevented complete healing in our society. But we shouldn't start without a clear line of approach. I wouldn't send you into this process without appropriate tools of support.

This book provides a structure to begin meaningful conversations about race, culture, bias, privilege, and power, given the limited time constraints of an ordinary learning institution. With most activities typically requiring between 12 and 30 minutes, a team of educators could reasonably build a fundamental understanding of the influence of race and culture in educational institutions through the course of four quarters or a year.

The first three chapters of the book lay the groundwork for introducing and implementing an initiative on disrupting inequity. By examining most resistance factors to dialogues on race, you can plan ahead of time how you will confront each and every one.

Chapter 1, "The Case for Cultural Competency," provides an evidence-based rationale for implementing this work in schools. Chapter 2, "Dismantling Inequity: Leading the Change," offers strategies for preparing for the change. Chapter 3, "When Silence Abounds: Facilitating Race Discussions Successfully," provides guidance on facilitating complex conversations.

In Chapters 4 through 7, you'll find activities for conversations on equity that build cultural competency during each of the four quarters of the school year. These four chapters also tackle the four main sets of actions educators need to take to become culturally competent. You'll begin your work in Chapter 4, "Awaken and Assess," learning about yourself, your culture, and how it influences your personal and professional behavior. Chapter 5, "Apply and Act," will guide you as you adapt your professional practices to meet the needs of all your students. In Chapter 6, "Analyze and Align," you'll look at policies and practices that inhibit opportunity for marginalized populations, and you'll explore how to align resources to eradicate inequity in your school. Finally, in Chapter 7, "Advocate and Lead," you'll learn how to advocate for equitable access and opportunities for all.

Designed for integration into grade-level, staff, content specialist, district, or school board meetings, the exercises in these four chapters are intentionally short and intense, with deep critical thinking opportunities to be conducted sometimes individually but most times in pairs or small groups. (Additional homework handouts are found in a separate section near the end of the book.) Following each exercise, participants are strongly encouraged to probe the content deeper with related research-based articles. Recommendations are provided that provide greater insight, context, and background to topics. Please don't discount the importance of further reading to build knowledge and understanding. It is integral to building cultural competency. At the end of each quarter, there is an interactive scenario for participants to read and discuss that applies the major concepts introduced in that quarter. The scenarios foster rich conversation on how certain behaviors manifest themselves in the workplace and how participants might respond. The eighth and last chapter, "The Long Road Ahead," offers recommendations for sustaining this work, suggesting ways to create more equitable and inclusive schools.

The Time Is Now

As a nation, we know how to progress. I have seen it firsthand, as have so many of my contemporaries. As evidence, my meager stories about inequity in schools *pale* in comparison to my father's. He could recall times when school leaders darkened the auditorium lights as students of color received their diplomas, when students could be beaten for speaking their native tongue, when students of color yearned for the right to visit the local library, and when mere association with a white person could result in imprisonment, mutilation, or death. Although these dark days are behind us, the prejudicial narratives that served to justify these actions live on through institutional and systemic racism.

In a popular U.S. television program, *The Walking Dead*, a man awakens from a coma to find his world overtaken by zombies. These *walkers* believe that most people are their enemy. Their behavior is dictated by a subconscious quest to attack people who look different from themselves.

Similarly, the legacy of our complex past has made for a current society of walkers who have subconsciously internalized ideologies, assumptions, and beliefs about people that are different from them. They often operate on auto play. Without questioning the origin of their ideas, exploring their cognizant actions, understanding the roots of the policies they employ, and mining the influence of pervasive and negative media messaging, some educators are stalking, attacking, and destroying the ambitions of people of color. The result is the perpetuation of educational, social, and economic injustice they claim to be against. And another generation of children are watching, listening, and emulating what they see. Let's provide a different social and cultural legacy for them than the one we inherited.

I long for the day when stories of inequity in schools seem foreign, antiquated, and even barbaric. When people gasp at the innocence and ignorance of a bygone time where people worked side by side without understanding one another, when characterizing a person based on the melanin in their skin seems as absurd as using leeches to cure the common cold. I have every faith in our ability as educators to place this matter of achievement and discipline gaps in the annals of history, along with our complex past. It can only begin, however, with the willingness, ability, and skills to understand both ourselves and one another.

I believe Julian Weissglass (2001) said it best when he wrote,

> If, as a nation, we develop communities in which people can speak honestly and productively about racism and heal from its hurts, we can change biased practices and attitudes. If we can communicate love and caring to all our students and help them recover from racism and internalized racism, they will be much more likely to achieve their full academic potential. If we do all this, we will accomplish more than reducing the achievement gap. We will create a better society. (p. 49)

I'm all for that. Let the cultural competency conversations begin!

1

The Case for Cultural Competency

There are few things more frustrating than being misunderstood. Imagine having your intentions questioned every time you walk into a room, make a purchase, or drive down the street; your humanity questioned and assessed like a relentless pop quiz; your successes met with disbelief, anger, or denial. Imagine having every behavior, emotion, nuance, and physicality scrutinized, labeled, criticized, demonized, criminalized, or mocked—at times with clear intention and other times with complicit indifference. Imagine having your aspirations mocked, your progress chastised, your self-worth ridiculed, your identity deprived, your accomplishments minimalized, your culture bastardized, your talents narrowly defined, and your intellect derided. Without a word, you are deemed a menace as peers shrink away in fear or stare with indignance.

Such are the experiences of many people of color who live their lives being misunderstood. How did things get this way?

Students of Color in Public Schools (This Isn't Pretty)

The American social, economic, and educational system was intentionally designed to have a ruling elite class and a subservient class destined to serve them (Apple, 2009; Watkins, 2001). To educate everyone equally would have been counterproductive to a socioeconomic structure in which power, wealth, and status were granted on the basis of your ability to assimilate within a dominant class. The dominant class, whose domination was established by brutal force and the crafting of clever narratives to deflect from that force, established schooling for their children while initially denying schooling for all others. Like so many policies that guided the establishment of America, keeping the perceived underclass in ignorance was legislatively established and legally enforced (Abul, 2008). Teaching a person of color to read or write could result in severe fines or imprisonment if the perpetrator was white. Whippings or worse punishments were rendered if the perpetrator was Black (Blackmon, 2009; King, 2005).

During the period of slavery in America, educated African Americans were a novelty. The educated few, however, were powerful and compelling rebuttals to the narrative of white supremacy. Their voices resounded with bitter clarity the evils of institutional racism, and many were active in the abolitionist movement (Lerone, 1975).

After emancipation, African Americans did not fare better in terms of educational opportunity. Many whites still opposed the education of ex-slaves (Hart, 2002). Schools that did so were burned and their teachers threatened, and any person of color who demonstrated agency, resolve, dignity, or intellect was often summarily murdered or lynched (Watson, 2012). These kinds of intimidating practices imparted fear, distrust, and a legacy of generational trauma among African Americans that is still evidenced in modern-day behaviors.

There were few exceptions, but most notable were the Rosenwald Schools, the brainchild of Tuskegee Institute's Booker T. Washington and Julius Rosenwald, an American businessman and philanthropist. Nearly 5,000 schools were built in the U.S. rural South to educate poor Black children. The schools were built with modern architectural features and admitted generous natural light, but they lacked updated textbooks, materials, and resources, which exacerbated an already growing gap between academic quality measures in Black and white schools (Carruthers & Wanamaker, 2013). The teachers, however, promoted a rigorous curriculum and encouraged the students to achieve at high levels. Some of the distinguished alumni include Maya Angelou and Representative John Lewis of Georgia.

In 1896, Plessy v. Ferguson ruled that public facilities, such as schools, that were separated by race were legal if they were equal. Alleged separate but equal educational institutions were established for minorities. These schools were often controlled with the hegemonic values and beliefs of white superiority. The dominant class largely wrote the curriculum in which the ingenuity, intellect, tenacity, and accomplishments of people of color were deliberately omitted. The curriculum, resources, and facilities for people of color were conveniently inferior to those available to the dominant class (Cross, 2007). The culture, values, and identity of people of color were denigrated and negatively dictated. Cultural repression was leveraged within the education system to make the oppressed ashamed of themselves, their values, and their history (Lerone, 1975).

Meanwhile, white scientists conducted studies theorizing that people of color were biologically and cognitively inferior to whites. This kind of rationalization of Black intellectual inferiority provided a framework for the denial of social privileges during the 20th century and rationalized the colonial plundering of their assets, economic domination, and denial of equitable educational opportunities (Watkins, 2001).

Postsecondary institutions for Black people also differed vastly from their white counterparts (Condron, 2009; Lerone, 1975). First, they were structured to be highly regimented. Students were expected to adhere to a strict course of discipline. (If that sounds eerily familiar to you, you might want to reexamine the discipline policy in your school.) Black people were taught how to cook, clean, perform physically challenging work, and do mentally menial tasks (Watkins, 2001). Schools that chose to deviate from the established curriculum by offering courses in the hard sciences were denied funding from their wealthy white benefactors (Anderson, 1980). The goal for Black education was to create an obedient and stable semiskilled workforce (Hart, 2002). According to Darder (2002), education was thus used as an "institutionalized politicizing process for conditioning students to subscribe to the dominant ideological norms and political assumptions of the prevailing social order" (p. 156).

During the Jim Crow years, institutions such as Harvard or Columbia admitted and graduated limited numbers of Black students, but those students were typically barred from teaching in these institutions. And although some Black students attended classes along with white students, they were usually prevented from using the campus libraries and laboratories or attending scholarly association meetings.

After World War II, the G.I. bill provided all veterans with eligibility for low-cost mortgages, low-cost loans to start a business, and tuition and living expenses to attend college. The bill also entitled veterans to receive one year of unemployment compensation. Although responsible for creating an American middle class, the bill also created the largest divide in economic status between whites and people of color. G.I. bill grants were distributed to states and local agencies, including those that practiced Jim Crow laws (laws that supported American apartheid). Thus, many soldiers of color were denied access to the funds. Even though they had served their country in the same way as all other soldiers, they were unable to advance economically, as the white soldiers did. People of color were denied well-paying jobs, retirement pensions, competitive educational degrees, and business capital—all of which resulted in their inability to gain middle-class status as easily as their white counterparts.

Soldiers of color who *were* granted access to G.I. funding pursued education but were limited in their choices. Not all colleges and universities accepted people of color, and those that did limited the number of slots available. Historically Black colleges and universities accepted students, but they were not as numerous as white institutions.

Veterans of color who were granted G.I. funds for housing were limited in where they could purchase a home. Certain neighborhoods prevented the sale of homes to people of color. The mortgage industry redlined areas where people of color lived and made it difficult for them to get reasonable mortgage rates or lines of credit. Schools in the redlined neighborhoods were crippled with inferior levels of funding and quality of education. As Watkins (2001) stated, "Black education experienced a separate tradition in funding, administration, teacher training, and curriculum" (p. 180). The inability to advance economically through home ownership or quality education prevented many people of color from pursuing postsecondary education.

By the end of the 1940s, the National Association for the Advancement of Colored People (NAACP) began a class action suit for the integration of schools, which ended with a 1954 U.S. Supreme Court decision (Brown v. Board of Education) to abolish segregated schools with "deliberate speed" (King, 2005, p. 157). This legislation, however, did little to sway public opinion about integrating schools, and many districts simply ignored the mandate (Atkinson, 1993). In 1957, President Dwight Eisenhower was forced to send federal troops to ensure the personal security of nine students determined to integrate Central High School in Arkansas. Additional support for desegregating schools would arrive in the form of the Civil Rights Act of 1964, which provided financial assistance to schools and districts attempting to desegregate.

President Lyndon Johnson's declaration in 1964 of an unconditional war on poverty in America was followed by one of the most influential pieces of educational legislation in American history—the Elementary and Secondary Education Act (ESEA) of 1965 (Haycock, 2006). This bill would more than triple the amount of federal dollars allocated to support poor citizens in public school systems, many of whom were people of color. Supported by mandated busing, people of color began integrating into educational institutions at an increasing rate (Atkinson, 1993).

When President Johnson signed an executive order for affirmative action, many white colleges and universities began actively recruiting minorities and offering financial assistance. Consequently, enrollment of minorities increased in colleges and universities across the United States.

However, by the mid-1960s and early 1970s, disturbing trends and patterns emerged. White families began to flee districts that were forced to integrate schools. National Assessment of Educational Progress (NAEP) tests in reading and math confirmed that minority children were not performing as well academically as their white counterparts in both lower-income and middle-class schools (Raffel, 1980). If that wasn't alarming enough, in 1972, the National Education Association reported that Black children were being pushed out of school, suspended, harassed, and arrested. African American students in desegregated schools were systematically excluded from extracurricular activities, tracked into vocational classes, and confronted with condescension or hostility (Atkinson, 1993). Twenty-five years after Brown v. Board of Education, school desegregation was briefly achieved. However, equity and the underlying beliefs enabling it had not withstood the trial (Atkinson, 1993).

Incentivized Achievement

The unfunded No Child Left Behind Act of 2001 (NCLB) legislated schools and districts to examine the achievement of minority subgroups in schools (Haycock, 2006). However, this legislation simplified the complexity of factors that brought education to this vortex (Bae, Holloway, Li, & Bempechat, 2008). Few questioned the deeply ingrained belief systems of teachers and staff who were now teaching diverse student populations (Berliner, 2010).

During fiscal year 2009–2010, the Obama administration allocated an unprecedented amount of stimulus dollars for school reform (McGuinn, 2012). For the first time in U.S. history, schools would be given both the ideals of equity and excellence in schools *and* the financial support to achieve them.

Over $7 billion was allocated for turning around chronically low-performing schools and supporting innovation through a program titled Race to the Top, which incentivized educational innovation.

Grant recipients crafted school improvement plans designed to address academic achievement gaps, yet few schools used the monies to help teachers understand minority students and the families with whom they had little interaction in their social or private lives. Thus, many educators were endeavoring to close achievement gaps that they could neither define nor explain (Andrews, 2007). Schools with high minority student populations worked tirelessly to address teacher shortages and high staff turnover, but few used the grant monies to address the influence of their students' culture in the environment—a phenomenon that greatly influenced teacher retention, as teachers were often baffled by the seemingly odd behaviors of their minority students (Allen, 2008; Ford & Moore, 2013).

Teachers and faculty largely ignored race, privilege, and inequity while seeking to improve schools through strict and regimented systems that privileged some, disciplined most, and disenfranchised others (Hart, 2002; Howley, Woodrum, Burgess, & Rhodes, 2009). School staff claimed color blindness while simultaneously instituting policies and programs that perpetuated the inequitable suspension and expulsion of minority children. Staff convened around improving schools and student learning while largely ignoring the effect of culture, poverty, generational trauma, violence, poor nutrition, and an absence of regular health care on the students they were serving (Day-Vines & Day-Hairston, 2005; Epstein, Galindo, & Sheldon, 2011; Gay, 2002; Ware, 2006; Weinstein, Curran, & Tomlinson-Clarke, 2003).

Dismantling Inequity for Improved Outcomes

Creating equitable educational opportunities for all has been an espoused goal of American educational policy since 1954 (Blackmore, 2009). But history has demonstrated that the ability to achieve it will take more than legislation (Orfield & Eaton, 1996). We tried desegregation. We tried busing. We tried testing. We tried financial support. What we have *not* tried with reasonable effort, intention, and consistency is confronting the values and beliefs that established inequity as a way of life in America.

What we're afraid to talk about is how race has been used to establish economic and educational advantage for a ruling class while perpetuating economic and educational subservence for others. What don't we want to talk about? How we, as educators, treat children and their parents who look, act, and behave differently than we do. What are we avoiding in school improvement planning? The examination of practices and policies that perpetuate privilege and benefits for some while disadvantaging others. Too often when the history of educational racism in this country is presented to many educators, they plug their fingers in their ears, close their eyes, and endeavor to drown out the hum of pain from the oppressed.

Some educators blame the victims and point to the current circumstances of the victims as somehow being their own fault, rather than examine the mare's nest of deliberate havoc that created those circumstances. More than ever, we need an army of educators with the political, moral, and professional will to dismantle systems of oppression that have historically crippled opportunity and access for students of color. We need champions of children who are willing to be temporarily uncomfortable so that all children might be enduringly celebrated and educated equitably. We need advocates for educational advancement who are willing to examine themselves, their behaviors, and their values as part of school improvement efforts. We need culturally competent educators. We need you.

Cultural competency, as I define it, is *the ability to use critical-thinking skills to interpret how cultural values and beliefs influence conscious and unconscious behavior; the understanding of how inequity can be and has been perpetuated through socialized behaviors; and the knowledge and determined disposition to disrupt inequitable practices to achieve greater personal and professional success for yourself and others* (Clark, Zygmunt, & Howard, 2016; Gay, 2010; Howard, 2010).

To examine this definition more closely, culture, as defined by Howard (2010), is "a complex constellation of values, mores, norms, customs, ways of being, ways of knowing, and traditions that provide a general design for living, is passed from generation to generation, and serves as a pattern for interpreting reality" (p. 51). Culture, therefore, influences how people think, the decisions they make, how they learn, what they believe is important to learn, how they speak, how they dress—in a nutshell, the values, beliefs, and behaviors on which they operate daily. We learn cultural values, mores, norms, and ways of being through people around us, media messages, common events, celebrations, and observances. We are immersed in a culture, sometimes several at once, from the time we are born until the time we die. Some of the behaviors, values, and beliefs we hold are conscious to us and espoused with regularity. Sometimes they are unconscious to us; they have become such a part of our belief system that we operate on them without critically examining why.

I prefer the term *cultural competence* to *antiracist education* because it embodies the comprehensive nature of culture, which is inclusive of the multiple identities one assumes or nurtures. The culture of an individual is complex in terms of what people learn or reject within their environment, including factors such as implicit bias, racism, privilege, and identity. The term *competence* suggests that you are endeavoring to become fluent in a set of practices or skills that advance your professionality. We are all competent in something. We can be competent in understanding cultural influences and challenging ones that are socially unjust.

Understanding how we are socialized through culture and subcultures is a distinctive knowledge set. Knowing how to examine those cultural values and beliefs as they manifest in school settings and dismantle the practices that perpetuate inequity is a level of competency that all educators need in order for students to succeed. It is possible to learn how to do this. And that is what this book is about.

As a young mother, I was eating an ice cream cone with my sons when I bit down to the bottom of the cone and threw it away. "Why did you do that?" J.R. asked me. "Do what?" I retorted. "Throw the bottom of your cone away, Mom. Why do you do that?" I paused for a moment and had to think about it. As a child, my aunt had worked at an ice cream cone factory in the 1950s and would never eat the bottom of the cone. She swore it to be unsanitary. We were never allowed to do so either. Twenty years later, my lips had never touched the bottom of a cone, and I was operating on autopilot.

Don't laugh too hard. There are things you have done without thinking about them, too. There are beliefs you hold that influence the decisions you have made—some of them made on autopilot as well. If you can understand how the messages you receive, both verbal and nonverbal, influence the things you do, you can comprehend the importance of culture in both teaching and learning. Cultural competency, therefore, prompts you to examine the cultural values that are influencing people's behavior. You must understand your own values and beliefs, but it is important for you to also understand the cultural values and beliefs of your students. When the messages people have received result in behaviors that perpetuate inequity within our society (and many of them do), a culturally competent educator moves into action, disrupting practices that advantage some and disadvantage others.

Cultural competency is the calling of every reasonably competent educator who believes in the value of education to elevate everyone and who desires the critical skills to do so. Culturally competent educators are a positive, disruptive force; they construct the future through their actions and words. With an idealized vision of the future, they wield their knowledge and influence to challenge the normalization of oppression and examine their role in the system. They are willing to break down barriers to opportunities for historically underserved learners and create a generation of educated advocates.

What Knowledge, Skills, and Dispositions Do We Need?

Awakening the deeply embedded values and beliefs on which we are operating and *assessing* where we are, personally, in terms of cultural competency is the first step in becoming culturally competent. The second step is understanding the cultural, social, economic, and legislative environments that create and perpetuate a system of inequitable treatment, opportunities, and outcomes for groups of people with common physical characteristics and *applying and acting* on that knowledge to examine false narratives perpetuated within our cultural context. The third step is *analyzing* policies and practices for inequitable outcomes, elevating the humanity of everyone, alleviating the daily indignities suffered by oppressed populations, and *aligning* new policies and practices with resources. The final step is *advocating and leading*, as well as mentoring and sharing power with others, and collaboratively working with others to dismantle inequitable systems.

Don't get so caught up in the semantics of the term *cultural competency* that you minimize the scope of this work. It is justly grounded in culture because that is the context in which we learn and unlearn ideology and practices, but the outcome is educational justice, antiracist advocacy, and leadership for dismantling inequitable systems and practices. Culturally competent educators manifest discreet knowledge, skills, and dispositions as outlined in the Cultural Competency Continuum shown in Figure 1.1.

Do Racially/Ethnically Homogenous Schools Need Culturally Competent Teachers?

Yes, enthusiastically yes! And here's why: You can teach in a school with little or no racial or ethnic diversity and still have a culturally diverse student body. Race, after all, is merely a fluid, socially constructed way to identify which people will be granted power, influence, resources, and privileges and which ones will likely not. It has no biological basis, but there are vividly disparate

Figure 1.1 The Cultural Competency Continuum: Knowledge, Behaviors, and Dispositions for Educators

	Culturally competent professionals acknowledge and continually examine the influence of culture, race, power, and privilege and how that influence manifests itself in their personal and professional decisions.
STEP 1. AWAKEN AND ASSESS	_____I can recognize how past historical actions are affecting current social and economic circumstances. _____I am aware of my own values, beliefs, stereotypes, and biases. _____I can recognize how my cultural beliefs and biases may be affecting my decision making, behavior, and perceptions of others. _____I have unpacked my feelings about language acquisition, language barriers, and language bias and support linguistic diversity. _____I can recognize privilege in society and organizations. _____I understand how white privilege and racism affect me and others. _____I can identify and discuss several strengths of diverse culture, ethnicity, language, and identity. _____I understand the varied cultural values of my colleagues and students. _____I recognize the various kinds of racism. _____I understand the changing racial and ethnic demographics and am prepared to be culturally responsive to all of my students and colleagues. _____I understand the role of power in organizations and in the construction of race. _____I affirm and respect cultures other than my own. _____I value culture as an integral part of a person's identity and maintain cultural curiosity rather than fear or avoidance. _____I regularly and experientially explore the histories, accomplishments, interests, perceptions, and lived experiences of people of different cultural and racial identities. _____I actively seek to foster meaningful relationships with people of different cultural and racial identities.
	Culturally competent professionals recognize the relevance of culture and adapt professional practices to meet the needs of students from all backgrounds.
STEP 2. APPLY AND ACT	_____I regularly examine student data relative to gender, race, ethnicity, and language to monitor and manage equitable access and support services. _____I am intentional about incorporating relevant cultural knowledge into instruction, curriculum, resources, learning environment, outreach, and assessment. _____I use communication skills to facilitate, manage, and participate in discussions on race, culture, and difference. _____I help make all cultural groups feel welcomed and valued. _____I acknowledge, recognize, and seek diverse strengths among staff and students. _____I exercise strategies that create an inclusive, caring, and equitable environment. _____I identify, manage, and respond to cross-cultural conflict proactively and effectively. _____I regularly assess if my students feel respected and valued in class by asking them for feedback. _____I encourage students to raise my awareness by questioning biased assumptions or behaviors when observed in our school environment. Then I take action to positively address those assumptions or behaviors.

Culturally competent professionals analyze policies, procedures, and programs that inhibit access and opportunity for historically marginalized students and staff and align resources to eradicate inequity in the school community.

STEP 3. ANALYZE AND ALIGN

_____I know the legal issues surrounding racism, bullying, and fostering a hostile environment, and I examine policies and procedures to ensure my practices are fair and legally defensible.

_____I work with my colleagues to institutionalize our learning and implement agreed-on goals and vision.

_____I volunteer to work with colleagues in the selection of future personnel whose values align with the school's goals and vision—inclusive of increasing equity and access for students of color.

_____I volunteer to work with colleagues in aligning budgetary allocations with school goals and vision—inclusive of increasing equity and access for students of color.

_____I understand that my destiny is intertwined with the success or failure of all my students, and I work tirelessly to ensure that they are all successful.

_____I can effectively challenge racism, inequity, or discriminatory practices in a professional and proactive manner.

_____I own the responsibility for building an authentically inclusive and just classroom and school environment.

_____I empower parents to engage and lead.

_____I have critiqued various schoolwide policies and practices and worked to reduce or eliminate any that may perpetuate inequitable outcomes.

Culturally competent professionals have participatory, collaborative partnerships with stakeholders and are fervent advocates for equitable access and opportunities for all.

STEP 4. ADVOCATE AND LEAD

_____I reach out to parents and the community regularly and engage diverse stakeholders in the decision-making process for anything that affects them or the students.

_____I empower all stakeholders and encourage open dialogue and dissent.

_____I identify barriers that prevent certain populations from full access to services and have taught colleagues ways to remove them.

_____I confront racism when I see it.

_____I advocate for cultural competency and social justice effectively and professionally.

_____I reject any privileges that come with white racial identity and actively work to ensure everyone has equal access and opportunities.

_____I am a brave equity warrior. (And I've got the scars to prove it.)

social and economic outcomes for people with higher levels of melanin. Those outcomes and the systems, structures, institutions, or individuals who use their power to disproportionately and unfairly distribute opportunity, access, or resources to another based on their racial category are racist. Cultural competency can help one identify when racism is occurring because the design and infrastructure of social systems and institutions sustain or perpetuate it.

You need culturally competent educators because your school may have teachers and students who identify within identical racial categories and may seldom, if ever, face the emotional crush of racism, but the teachers may still grapple to understand the culture of the students and families at the school.

How does that happen? Culture—the shared values, beliefs, patterns, and communication styles of a group of people—has little to do with the amount of melanin in your skin. For example, a white person who grew up with a single parent in a small apartment in Aachen, Germany; a white person raised in a middle-class family in suburban Cabimas, Venezuela; and a white oil billionaire from Anchorage, Alaska, will likely have different values, beliefs, patterns, and communication styles. In fact, you are just as likely to find people who identify in the same racial background with dissimilar cultural values and beliefs as you are to find people who identify in the same racial categories with common cultural values and beliefs. The cultural values and beliefs you adopt are related to the messages you hear and learn about the world—what is important and what is not, who is important and who is not, things you should do and know and things you should not do or know, what is discussed and what is not, and so on. These messages are transmitted through your environment from parents, relatives, friends, media, school, and neighbors, to name a few. Sometimes they are communicated verbally, and other messages are observable through nonverbal behaviors.

Even then, culture is not static; it is an ever-evolving set of knowledge and beliefs evidenced through learned behavior and responses. You may move to a different community and adopt many of the practices, beliefs, values, or even communication styles of your new community that may conflict with previous beliefs. You may have life experiences that shift values and beliefs that you once held strongly.

There is also the issue of subcultures—cultural values that lie within very specific communities of larger cultural values. For example, if you live in the United States, there are common cultural values familiar to most residents.

If you live in the southern part of the United States, there are cultural values that are unique to that part of the country. And if you belong to a religious sect within that southern community, there are still other unique theological beliefs and values specific to the culture of that organization that guide you.

Organizations with minimal racial diversity still need culturally competent staff who can demonstrate their understanding of the historical context, nuances, and dynamics of various cultural values and who can demonstrate skills that create an optimal learning environment for students from all types of cultures. Racial identity is important, but it's not the only influence in understanding the cultures of people. If your school does not have a great amount of racial diversity, it can still benefit from staff who are culturally competent in understanding the cultures of their students and who know how to use that knowledge to craft better learning experiences for them.

Cultural competency is not the work of an elite band of educators who happen to work with populations that have a significant number of minority students and families. Teaching is not a spectator sport where we can afford to have educators stand at the sidelines observing a game that clearly favors some and disadvantages others, but who fail to get involved because it is not their team. All the students on the field are playing for their future *and yours*. They are the future voters and community members who will determine what resources are provided for your retirement, which people immigrate to your community, how crime and order will be managed, and how educators will be compensated. In short, they will make fundamental decisions about *your* quality of life. To underestimate or mismanage your responsibility as an educator is shortsighted at best and foolhardy at worst.

There is nothing passive or dispassionate about being a culturally competent educator. It has nothing to do with your race, ethnicity, culture, class, position, school location, or student population. Culturally competent educators recognize the power of their influence to change the course of history for the better, and they work collaboratively with colleagues to strategically critique where we failed in the past and where we'll endeavor to navigate in the future.

There is a long history of racial, gender, social, and cultural hierarchy of human value in our society (Alexander, 2010; Anyon, 1997). There are people who perpetuate the myth of racial superiority and actively work to preserve its legacy and economic privilege—some of whom may teach at your school.

As educators, we may have had no choice in how our society or school systems were constructed, but by our daily actions, we choose to perpetuate the existing system or redesign a better one. You can extend your influence beyond the boundaries of your classroom, school, or district. Exercising your talents through the lens of cultural competency is a vital tool in this effort.

Information is the currency of power, and schools are one of the social depositories that distributes or denies access to the currency. The more information one has, the more independent and autonomous a person becomes. Cultural competency is about distributing that currency equitably. Now, let's get to work!

2

Dismantling Inequity: Leading the Change

One of the first things I enjoyed doing as a new administrator at a school was to walk the facility alone before staff and faculty arrived, looking behind every door and into every closet, acquainting myself with the building and searching for signs of the hidden culture. I would usually find a back closet with equipment, textbooks, or supplies that had scarcely been used or were sometimes in their original wrappings. These sparkling new materials would be carefully buried in the back of a closet, whereas older, well-worn equipment, textbooks, and supplies were prominently on display.

Undoubtedly, many schools have a "change graveyard"—that place where new initiatives and their relics go to die. Somewhere along the road of change, an educator became discouraged with the process of implementation. Whatever they were asked to do, it stopped making sense. Perhaps they asked questions but lacked support. Perhaps the initiative was difficult to implement, made them feel uncomfortable, or lacked evidence that it was better than previous methods. Whatever the reason, at some point their questions were silenced or unanswered, and they grew weary of trying. Before long, they quietly tucked the vestiges of change into a hidden corner in a closet and returned to doing things the way they had always been done. It was likely just easier.

Maybe you have seen failed initiatives in your career or your school houses its own graveyard of such relics. One way to avoid that is to consider at the outset some of the challenges one might face with this type of work and plan ahead for gaining momentum and sustaining change. Cultural competency is too important a change to leave its implementation to chance. If we do not prepare to manage the potential emotional, mental, and psychological fallout from probing issues of race and culture in multicultural spaces, participants could well grow weary. Before you know it, all efforts, resources, and materials are stashed in the bottom of someone's closet, and the school culture self-corrects to maintain the comforts and privileges of the status quo.

Time for an Honest Conversation

Many an educator has fallen prey to the waves of change and struggled for a lifeline to stay afloat. If you think it can be challenging to manage the implementation of a new curriculum or a highly politicized policy, consider dismantling systems, practices, and policies that are deeply steeped in people's cultural values and beliefs. Try challenging people's internalized narratives about people, institutions, and systems. Attempt to interrogate the values people embrace as part of their personal identities as Americans. Take a stab at critiquing beliefs instilled during the evening news or as a result of the continual onslaught of a lifetime's worth of negative media coverage. When you do, you may likely encounter a turbulence you didn't even realize was stirring beneath the generally calm waters of the school.

During World War II, more than half a million naval mines were dropped into the ocean. If triggered, they were designed to cause permanent and lasting damage to ships and potentially the loss of lives. These explosive devices buried deep on the ocean floor lay quietly dormant for years after the conflict. Above the surface, the ocean waves were calm and serene, but there were vast stretches of waters that if disturbed could erupt into a violent explosion.

Despite the precarious nature of the mission, naval personnel began to sweep the ocean floors for mines. It was not easy, and it took years of work. Many of the mines had been dropped by air and it was hard to determine exactly where they had landed or where undercurrents had taken them. The mines varied in size and weight. Some mines were quite small, while others quite large, yet all were dangerous and finding them was vital. Few, if any, of the navy officers assigned to this mission were responsible for dropping the mines, yet they worked tirelessly to alleviate future harm, damage, or loss of life. Their bravery was a testament to the fact that just because something may be challenging doesn't mean it shouldn't be done.

The United States dropped mines of a different sort on their own land and buried them deep within the soil. The violent takeover of Native American land. Bomb buried. The cruelty of human enslavement. Bomb buried. The forceful pilfering of Mexican homes, lands, and resources. Bomb buried. Black Wall Street burned to the ground. Bomb buried. Someone's grandfather burned and lynched. Bomb buried. Unarmed Black children stalked and executed in the streets. Bombs buried. The teacher next door who suffered an indignity this morning. Bomb buried. The social and economic subjugation, decriminalized murder, and oppression of people of color over the past 400 years. Bombs buried everywhere. As a country we have been tiptoeing around these mines for years. We know they are there. We know they exist. We know that people's lives have been irreparably changed, damaged, or lost as a result of them. We understand they have changed the trajectory of some people's futures. But we've managed to steer clear of those waters for many years. You or I may not have personally dropped any of these mines, but today we are going to start disarming them to alleviate future harm, damage, or loss of life. And we are going to start dismantling the systems that continue to allow them to be buried without accountability. It's a tedious task, but just because it is challenging doesn't mean it shouldn't be done.

I have personally navigated the murky waters of change while fighting strong cultural riptides in schools. At one time, I was a turnaround principal endeavoring to disrupt a culture that was steeped in mediocrity. Even with a distributed leadership model, the system "tsunamied" against the change, threatening to hurl us all into an uncertain storm. I learned some valuable lessons along the way.

Challenging the status quo, probing deeply rooted beliefs, and surfacing unconscious bias in an effort to transform the culture in schools and dismantle inequity need to be undertaken with prior thought and planning. Given my own experience as well as scholarship in the field, I offer six recommendations for how to best prepare yourself and your team for leading this change. These are not one-time events. Rather, they are actions and behaviors that need to be grounded in all your work moving forward and into the foreseeable future. They need to be embedded in the school culture to ensure the conversations continue and that you remain committed to growth. (1) *Establish* or revisit your school mission and vision and *set* goals. You will need to connect with something bigger than yourself to achieve great things and inspire others to do so as well. (2) *Create* a caring community. Within the context of a caring community, you are relatively unstoppable in meeting any challenge.

(3) *Communicate* your goals to stakeholders and help them understand the complexity of the work. Should you hit rough waters, it helps if you've already filed your travel log and stakeholders are aware of the potential climate forecast. (4) *Organize* for ongoing learning. You will need all hands on-deck. As educators, you hopefully understand the importance of building background knowledge to deepen understanding. This work is organized around collaborative learning groups, thought partners, and extensive reading and discussions outside of group meetings. Like any professional relationship, established norms and consistent meeting times are essential. (5) *Rethink, reframe, and redirect conflict.* Not just an elite few—everyone. The whole team should know how to deescalate a situation while continuing to navigate toward a determined goal. If you are disarming potential emotional bombs, you are going to need to think differently about conflict. (6) The final step is to *empower* each other for leadership, agency, and activism. The culturally competent educator is an active and vocal one. The nature of this work calls you to lead (Rivera-McCutchen, 2014). You can lead from the front, the side, or the back, but you're definitely going to stand out. Square your shoulders. Forward ho!

Step 1: Establish Vision and Set Goals

A number of researchers support the importance of establishing a vision of where you want to be before beginning a process of change (Finnigan & Stewart, 2009; Scribner & Reyes, 1999). How well does your school vision, mission, or school improvement plan connect to people emotionally? Is your mission statement aspirational? Does it promote ideology or goals that inspire? Does it connect stakeholders to a purpose that is bigger than themselves? Does it reflect what our stakeholders value? And is equity, fairness, or educational justice integral to what we say is important to our work? It may be difficult for you to gain traction on a schoolwide effort on cultural competency if the school mission is inconsistent with these goals. If giving all students a fair chance to succeed is not part of your school mission or vision, you need to rethink what you're doing and for whom. If your school vision and mission hasn't changed in the past 50 years, look around. Your students, community, social culture, and the world around you has changed. Why shouldn't the mission keep pace? It may be time for a meaningful discussion with stakeholders that acknowledges some students' needs are simply greater than others. What commitment or agreements can be made to address them? Laying the groundwork with these kinds of discussions is crucial and will make the work go far smoother once some fundamental acknowledgments are agreed upon.

Consider at the outset how you will frame the urgency of this work as you communicate and discuss it among yourselves. By helping one another understand the overall vision of the impact of this work, you will achieve a higher level of commitment for continuing through the messiness of change.

What About Core Values?

The school mission and vision are grounded in the community's core values. All too often, we establish core values for schools and prominently display them on a plaque or poster in the main office or hallway. Yet they're seldom discussed outside of disciplinary actions, if then. If you will take the time to interrogate why you are making the choices you are making and why we, as a collective team of educators, make the choices we make, you can begin to build both personal and collective resiliency when the work becomes stressful. Understand why you're taking these steps toward cultural competency and what you hope to accomplish. Then marry your personal core values to those of the school.

The thrust is twofold here. You should take each agreed-on core value and operationalize what it should look like when evidenced in your practice or the organization. You should also determine where cultural competency aligns with the core values, then make its presence explicit.

Being a culturally competent educator should align with everything you do and everything you are as an organization, or it will be seen as something else piled on an already full plate. Help colleagues connect the dots between the mission of the organization and the work of becoming culturally competent. Then when you experience challenges such as conflict, chaos, or fatigue, review the core values of the organization in relation to the work you are doing and help your colleagues frame them within the perspective of the larger work of the organization.

Core values are built on collective beliefs about how we will live and work together, what is important to us, and how those beliefs serve us in the mission of the organization. Operationalizing those values articulates a clear vision of what it looks like when we exercise the values and provides a vision of an ideal. Vision is so vital that Heifetz (1994) states you cannot claim to have a learning organization without one. As he notes,

> A common vision establishes an overarching goal for the hard work you are about to engage in. It continues to propel people forward despite the hardships involved. With a shared vision, we are more likely to expose our ways of thinking, give up deeply held views, and recognize personal and organizational shortcomings. All that trouble seems trivial compared with the importance of what we are trying to create. (p. 209)

Cultural Proficiency as a Continuum

Part of the vision-building process is assessing your starting point. With cultural competency everyone will not be starting from the same place. Lindsey, Robins, and Terrell (2003) describe cultural proficiency on a continuum (see Figure 2.1). At its lowest level, *cultural destructiveness*, one sees difference as a problem and identifies one culture as superior to others. The next level, *cultural incapacity*, perpetuates stereotypes and invokes a paternalistic attitude toward other nondominant groups. At the third level, *cultural blindness*, one does not believe culture accounts for differences or is of little value. At the fourth level, *cultural pre-competence*, one notices difference but chooses not to make changes or accommodations for them. At the fifth level, *cultural competence*, one accepts, appreciates, and values difference. One begins to seek out others with diverse opinions. Researchers define the highest level as *cultural proficiency*, in which individuals seek to help others less informed and regularly engage in interaction with diverse groups (Lindsey, Roberts, & CampbellJones, 2005; Lindsey et al., 2003). The framework shown in Figure 2.1 provides a visual portrait of the theoretical framework for cultural proficiency in which individuals progress along a continuum that ends in the ability to appreciate and champion differences in others.

Figure 2.1 **Cultural Proficiency Continuum**

Cultural Destructiveness	Cultural Incapacity	Cultural Blindness	Cultural Pre-Competence	Cultural Competence	Cultural Proficiency

Source: From *Cultural Proficiency: A Manual for School Leaders* (2nd ed.), (p. 54), R. B. Lindsey, K. N. Robins, and R. D. Terrell, 2003, Thousand Oaks, CA: Corwin.

White Racial Identity Development

Helms (1990; 1995) describes how white individuals evolve into racial allies by advancing through six statuses. In *contact* status, whites frequently deny racism exists; they avoid discussions of race and ignore instances of racist behaviors. During *disintegration* status, whites become aware that racism exists and disassociate with it personally, although they are reluctant to prevent or interrupt it. They begin to recognize that if they take a stand against the injustices done to others, it may compromise their own social status or privileges. The resulting internal conflict may pull them into a *reintegration* status where they can exist more comfortably. In this status, whites are aware of the injustices of racism, but they blame the victims for their plight. By doing so, they absolve themselves of the risks of abandoning practices that perpetuate racism, jeopardize their social standing, or threaten a personal identity they hold dearly. If they continue to examine themselves and how they see themselves in the world, they may enter *pseudo-independence* status, where they recognize their responsibility for dismantling systems and practices that are unfair to others. They may be unsure yet of how to proceed. In *immersion/emersion* status, whites begin to understand their privilege in society as a white person and are interested in redefining what it means to be a white person in this world. *Autonomy* status represents the final status in the White Racial Identity Development model; here, whites relinquish the privileges of racism and move to take action against it.

The statuses in this theoretical framework are not necessarily sequential; people can jump back and forth between statuses at any point in their development (Helms, 1992; Helms, 1995; Helms & Cook, 1999). This framework has proved useful to help some people examine and understand themselves and others.

Black Racial Identity Development

There are five stages in the Black Racial Identity Development process, according to Cross, Parham, and Helms (1991). In the *preencounter* stage, Black individuals internalize the negative narratives and stereotypes they have heard about people of color and have been socialized to believe that it is their role to assimilate into the dominant culture. They distance themselves from other Black people and work actively for acceptance from white people. Typically, people in this stage earnestly believe that race has little, if anything, to do with their achievement in society. They have fully bought the myths of meritocracy that propagandize the successes of others as having been granted solely due to their hard work and tenacity. This is not to negate these values entirely, but as we will learn, success in this society is disproportionately granted to people born with light skin. And although some worked hard to achieve success, none of them were denied reasonable access to an education, the ability to pursue their goals, or access to housing, jobs, or high-quality medical care because their skin was white.

Individuals will transition into the *encounter* stage when an event or learning experience awakens them to the realization that although they have imagined their racial identity made little difference to others, they now recognize it genuinely does. They come to the realization that they have not and will not be accepted equally by some white individuals. They now begin to position themselves as a member of a group that is the target of racism.

Cross presents that Black people in the *immersion/emersion* stage begin to identify with symbols of Black culture. There is an increased interest in learning about Black culture, history, and achievements. As they learn about all the ways racism has been perpetuated on people of color, anger or resentment toward white people may emerge, but it will eventually subside as they focus more on the accomplishments and history of Blacks that are a source of pride and engage with other Black individuals with shared experiences.

During the fourth stage, *internalization*, Black individuals have defined for themselves their racial identity. They maintain their Black friends or acquaintances but also reach out to white individuals who are respectful of their identity and experiences. They form alliances with other oppressed people.

In the final stage, *internalization-commitment*, Blacks see themselves and other people of color in a positive light. They identify positively as a Black person and are comfortable being their authentic selves. They understand the challenges that racism presents and prepare to advocate on behalf of oppressed people. They seek out opportunities to support people who are marginalized, advocate for their needs, and protest the inequities that have been maintained for generations (Cross et al., 1991). They see themselves as part of the solution to ending inequity.

Cultural Competency Continuum

The Cultural Competency Continuum introduced in Chapter 1 (see Figure 1.1, pp. 18–19) provides specific skills, knowledge, and dispositions that are critical for culturally competent educators. It can be both a pre- and post-assessment of skills and knowledge; the continuum will serve as our general guide throughout the activities. It is our roadmap for where we would ideally like to be as we work through our own individual continuums of growth.

It provides a baseline of where each person is starting. There are two ways to use this tool. You could simply place a check beside a knowledge, skill, or disposition (KSD) you believe you have mastered, or you could place a percentage next to the KSD. For example, if you believe you demonstrate a certain skill 10 percent of the time, you may choose to place a 10 beside it. By ranking yourself on a scale, you could evaluate your progress throughout the year or your career.

This tool is *not* an evaluative tool; it is not to be used for the purpose of evaluating a person professionally. The process of becoming culturally competent is very individual, and people progress at their own rates. There are other frameworks and tools that theorize other racial identities (Asian, indigenous, biracial, etc.), but the model, framework, and continuum presented here provide possible tools for gathering perspective on how individuals might assess their behaviors in relation to those of individuals who are deemed antiracist.

Step 2: Create a Caring Community

Many an initiative has gone awry because it was attempted in a toxic working environment. Motivation or innovation slow to a crawl in a culture of indifference or lack of support. The more distrust staff have in one another and in the leadership, the more likely they are to isolate themselves from others or fail to seek support when they struggle. On the other hand, people flourish, take acceptable risks, and grow in an environment where there is mutual trust among colleagues and people are respected for being their authentic cultural selves.

How do you achieve this? Within a caring environment. As you strive to better meet the needs of all students, remember that students and staff have fundamentally the same basic psychological needs, including the need to (1) be engaged in meaningful social relationships, (2) have autonomy and self-direction, and (3) feel efficacious in one's work (Olafsen, Deci, & Halvari, 2018). These needs can be met within a caring community.

Meaningful Social Relationships and Emotional Support Systems

All change involves an emotional component, and numerous scholars speak to the importance of paying attention to the thoughts, feelings, attitudes, and perceptions of the individuals experiencing and implementing change (Marzano, Waters, & McNulty, 2005). Issues centered on race, culture, privilege, and power are rooted in the ability of people to talk openly and honestly about these topics in multiracial, multicultural contexts. This is generally not taught in most educator preparation programs, not discussed in most white families, not mentioned in mentoring programs, avoided in staff meetings, and whispered in hushed tones among many educators of color. It would be a mistake to underestimate the complexity of introducing this variable into a significant change initiative. Although this is discussed more deeply in the next chapter, here are some concrete suggestions for creating institutionalized structures that allow people to check in with one another individually, collectively, and voluntarily. They also provide ways for people to feel connected and build meaningful social relationships.

- Ask people to select a thought partner for discussions, questions, and follow-up processing of ideas.
- Encourage the use of journaling.
- Establish small groups, pairs, or teams for group study or reading of related articles, materials, and information.
- Help people self-select mentors or professional guides.
- Create internal pen pals among staff.
- Design a fairy godmother or fairy godfather program where the goal is to have another staff member support the well-being of another, as needed. (At the end of the year, you may choose to invite everyone to a ball!)
- Have regular Lunch and Learn follow-up discussions on topics discussed or articles mutually read. Perhaps a local restaurant might be willing to underwrite these meetings with donated or inexpensive meals.
- Begin a school-level approach of "paying it forward." Do random acts of kindness for someone else once a week.
- Set up a compliment or thank you box, and have each person send an anonymous or signed compliment or note of thanks to one person each week. Then deliver the compliment mail at staff or grade-level meetings.
- Have staff members take personality tests, and display the results in the staff lounge. Let others see colleagues with whom they share common personality traits or interaction styles.
- Arrange days where people can get to know their colleagues' family members, such as Take Your Child to Work Day or Bring Your Spouse/Partner/Roommate to Work Day.
- Be the cheerleader for the shy, the newly hired, and the oddly gifted. Encourage acceptance and belonging of all stakeholders, even the most seemingly difficult.

Autonomy and Self-Direction

How do you inspire trust? You share leadership with others (Drescher, Korsgaard, Welpe, Picot, & Wigand, 2014). In a study of more than 140 groups during a four-year period, Drescher and colleagues (2014) found that shared leadership played a critical role in increasing levels of trust among team members. This dynamic occurs even when group members are engaged in different responsibilities, skills, and resources. Providing members autonomy and self-direction through shared leadership roles inspires trust and helps people feel valued. Here are some recommendations for fostering autonomy, self-direction, and leadership:

- Form a book club on educational equity topics. Take turns facilitating the group.
- Provide an opportunity for secondary school staff to learn firsthand the challenges and privileges of delivering different curricula. Have a Switch Roles Day; allow staff to select anyone in the school who is willing to switch roles with them for the day—including leadership.
- We often ask students to track the books they have read all year. How about staff? Keep a log in the lounge of interesting books staff members have read. Place a sticker next to the titles they recommend.
- Lunches, dinners, retreats, conferences, and holiday parties are ripe work for those who are detail-oriented and who enjoy coordinating and planning engaging events. Have folks sign up for supporting and planning the events.
- Have staff design a professional development day and deliver content.
- Rotate the facilitation of cultural competency exercises amongst staff volunteers.
- Adopt an attitude of inquiry and an expectation that everyone will learn. As a learning community, accept the fact that you can learn something from everyone you meet, from anyone with whom you interact, and from daily experience. The common question of "What did you learn today?" or "What did you learn this week?" can apply to every staff member. They might share their responses at team meetings, with students, or in a staff chat room.

Overall, staff need to believe they will be fully supported in their work; such support may include data, mentoring or guidance, leadership, and a purposeful collaborative culture (DeLuca, Bolden, & Chan, 2017; Nelson, Deuel, Slavit, & Kennedy, 2010; Sergiovanni, 2004).

Promote Efficacy

Everyone wants to feel competent in their work role. That may present more of a challenge during equity work and can have a deleterious effect when people grow weary of the enormous content they are consuming.

Flynn (2015) termed it *white fatigue*. It is defined as a temporary state in which white learners who intuitively embrace the moral imperative of anti-racism become fatigued or "tired of talking" about racism. According to Flynn, the problem is further aggravated by the person's concern with not being judged as racist if they voice how they feel. Sure, the team might begin with earnest intentions, but as time wears on, some learners may grow weary of issues that they feel have already been resolved or challenge their competency as antiracists. Before long, what should be open dialogue can devolve into mumbles, whispers, coffee break mutters, and parking lot venting.

To be fair, when this occurs, many learners (1) may recognize there is racism, (2) don't seem to see that there is much they can do about it, and (3) conceive of racism as individual acts of which they are not a part. Given that simplistic framework, it would hardly seem necessary to them to keep revisiting the issue. At this point, however, it is absolutely crucial to push through the curriculum to analyze the more complex nature of systemic, structural, and institutional racism; the larger role schools have played in perpetuating it; and the specific actions we can take to create more just and equitable systems and institutions.

Racism is a complex issue, and it is challenging at times to grapple with one's contribution—both past and present—to perpetuating inequitable outcomes while still maintaining a comfortable existence and conscience. Some personal and internal emotional struggles will likely result. They may surface as frustration or resignation toward topics of equity, race, culture, or privilege and are typically seen among individuals who initially committed to the process of discussing these issues but who did not have a clear understanding of the emotional toll that might accompany the experience.

If you see one of your colleagues slipping into this state, I recommend referring them to a trusted peer mentor who is willing to spend some time listening empathetically without judgment while holding fast to the long-term goals and vision of the organization.

One thing is certain. The process of adopting new ways of thinking can be emotionally taxing as people navigate through a process of letting go of old ways of thinking and embracing new ways. Don't let this take the change off track, however. It generally is temporary and can be overcome if people feel like they are not being forcefully silenced or negatively labeled for struggling through the process.

Supportive relationships are the foundation of a caring community, and they are indispensable to fostering an environment in which individuals' beliefs, perceptions, judgments, and practices are continually under critique and self-evaluation. Here are some other suggestions for helping each other promote competency:

- Encourage your colleagues to contribute at meetings. If you notice someone has not participated in a conversation, ask for their opinion and withhold judgment; be open to new ideas.

- If you are facilitating a meeting, distribute discussion questions in advance so people can have time to think about them and be prepared to discuss them. Ask others attending the meeting to distribute their questions, if any, ahead of time to help you feel better prepared to respond to questions.

- Express your willingness to help others using your professional expertise or on the basis of your interests.

- Give your colleagues positive feedback when you observe them doing things that align with the core values and beliefs of the organization. Pat folks on the proverbial back frequently.

- Speak well of your colleagues to leaders at the school, district, and community levels. Refuse to engage in petty gossip that leads to gross distrust. If you have concerns, take them to the individual in question and express your concerns with kindness.

- Allow staff members to identify their areas of expertise in an "expertise tree" so people begin to use the expertise of staff for additional information or support.

- Recognize staff birthdays with professional resources from their personal work wish lists.

- Create your own version of Academy Awards, and recognize every staff member for their unique contribution during the year or their professional contribution to students' academic success. You can have a lot of fun with this at the end of a school year by holding the event in a special location or crafting your own papier-mâché statues made by students.

You may need to be reminded why you decided to take on this challenge. When you do, I encourage you to hold on and see it through. Creating a caring community will be a work in progress that must be nurtured every day. It will be rewarding, however, to watch relationships strengthen, trust build, leadership flourish, and self-efficacy grow. It may well be the most rewarding professional experience of your career.

Step 3: Communicate Your Goals to Stakeholders

As a pilot it is standard practice to file a flight plan in advance of your travels. Typically, information included would be the type of aircraft, your proposed altitude and airspeed, and your departure and destination locations. The purpose of such a document is for your benefit: If you fail to reach your destination, it supports search and rescue operations.

Similarly, leaving a trip plan with a friend is highly advisable for long distance boating adventures. Someone should know the name and number of your vessel, the size and type of vessel you are traveling in, and other critical information such as the type of engine and radio channels you will be monitoring. Again, the purpose in sharing this information before you leave is that you want your support members to be apprised of where you are and when to intervene if you need additional help and support.

As you begin the journey toward cultural competency, inform all stakeholders of your intentions, your purpose, how that purpose aligns with the larger goal and vision at the school and district levels, and the possible emotional or psychological repercussions of advancing through this kind of change. Why? If the seas get rocky, some of your team members may send up flares prematurely. Other team members may contemplate a coup. And yes, some team members may even threaten to jump overboard. This kind of potential turmoil might be alarming to other stakeholders such as district personnel, the school board, parents, the community, or even students, if not for your preemptive insight in communicating your course, framing your message for each of the stakeholders, and providing a potential climate forecast before you leave port. Which stakeholders are early adopters and will readily get on board with a focus on equity? Which ones may resist all efforts? How do you converge the interests of competing parties and communicate that positively? In Capper's (2015) analysis of critical race theory in empirical studies about educational leadership, she found it was vital for leaders to thoughtfully frame their equity initiatives for white parents: "If leaders expect their equity efforts to be successful, their work must be framed in such a way that middle- and upper-class Whites in the community will also benefit; otherwise, White families will believe the racial equity work is not worth doing" (p. 814). You may need to craft a slightly different message for each stakeholder and help them understand how their interests and needs can be met while our most vulnerable populations are also getting their needs met. Plan ahead.

All stakeholders also need to understand the implications of the change process before you leave on this journey and the potential for feelings of conflict or chaos. Fullan (2005) argues that without change knowledge, any initiative you attempt may be doomed for failure. He notes, "Making change work requires the energy, ideas, commitment, and ownership of all those implementing improvements" (p. 55). It is continual, consistent learning and application of the learning through measurable actions (Fullan, 2005).

Stated another way, implementing this change is a learning process that is contextual to your specific school, population, staff, and circumstances. You are about to engage in a journey in which you will learn from yourself, learn from others, and learn from scholarly work. You will then translate that learning into actionable goals and targets. Together you will learn what is impeding equitable access, opportunity, and the positive, holistic development of every student in your school. Then you will fix it so it works. Sometimes the impeding force might be a policy, a practice, a procedure, an environment, and so on. Sometimes an impeding force might be . . . you—your language, your intonation, your approach, your instruction, your beliefs, your cultural values, your attitude, your bias, your prejudice, your racism, and so on. If you think that this is hard to read, consider how difficult it may be to do. Yet, whatever we discover through this process, we can surely fix for the sake of children and their futures. Buckle up, we might encounter turbulence. This is why we communicate consistent, thorough, and targeted messages to all of our publics.

Despite your best efforts, there may be some level of chaos, confusion, or erroneous conjecture that occurs as you grapple with the examination of beliefs and values that have never been critically examined before. Your stakeholders need to understand it is all part of the change process. Invite them to join you for the exercises if they have questions. Share the data you have collected that provide evidence of the need and urgency to address this issue. Assign several trusted point people who can be contacted if someone has questions. Schedule times to provide regular updates to the school board or district personnel on your progress.

What you do *not* need is a reactionary response resulting from misinformation that derails your hard work and efforts. Talk to parents, community members, and students. They may be interested in forming their own cohort of learners. On parent nights or during promotion events and community gatherings, create a booth that informs stakeholders of the goal, the process, and the journey. Communicate, communicate, and overcommunicate to your publics, preparing them for a disruption of the existing culture but also for the excitement of more inclusive and equitable outcomes for the school community.

Step 4: Organize for Ongoing Learning

Establish a regular time for discussing equity and for participating in the activities included in Chapters 4 through 7 to build cultural competency. If you already have a regular staff or grade-level team meeting time, it may be easier to incorporate discussions into that time slot. Start small, with 10 to 15 minutes dedicated to learning and growth in this area—and guard that time religiously. By allocating time and providing dedicated opportunities for discussions, you are establishing an important component of a collaborative and inclusive school culture.

Do not skip the reflective dialogue questions at the end of the exercises or the homework assignments in which you discuss your learning in depth with a critical friend. These are essential to processing the information, providing opportunity for staff to seek peer support, reflecting on individual understandings, and achieving new patterns of coherence.

I prefer to have discussions in a circle where everyone can be seen. This promotes a sense of community and inclusivity that does not allow most people to emotionally opt out of participation. Some people may look visibly uncomfortable within this structure. It is not a deal breaker, but nonparticipation should be. Reject endeavors by some to multitask other work during the dialogic learning exercises. The exercises in building cultural competency are not for spectators. We need the full engagement of all participants for the duration of the activity.

Step 5: Rethink, Reframe, and Redirect Conflict

As a high school administrator, our goal was to have each student connect with a caring adult. Each individual on the staff was assigned two students to mentor. One of my mentorees was an 18-year old man whom I'll call Carlos. Carlos was a single father of two toddlers. He lived at home with his mother, who watched and cared for his children. After a full day of classes, Carlos would report to work at a local auto supply store and work until midnight. Despite that hectic schedule, Carlos would faithfully attend school every day . . . an hour late. And his first hour teacher wasn't having it. "I'm trying, but I can't make it here by seven, Miss," he groaned to me as he lamented the verbal scolding he had just endured by his math teacher. "Will you talk to Mr. Caesar for me, please? I need this class to graduate, and it's the only one that doesn't conflict with my other classes." I sat there trying to figure out how I was going to support Mr. Caesar, who likely was trying to uphold high expectations for everyone, while also supporting Carlos, who was unlikely to make that attendance bar. I agreed to advocate on his behalf and braced myself for the conflict.

Conflict, in most work environments, is typically something we try to avoid. But sometimes, in order to accomplish a goal, you must confront it head on. Kerry Patterson, Joseph Grenny, Ron McMillan, and Al Switzler have numerous recommendations in their best-selling book *Crucial Conversations* (2012). I will highlight several I used with my dilemma.

Both parties at the heart of the conflict had framed the resolution as either/or. For Mr. Caesar: "Either you get to class on time *or* you will fail the class." For Carlos: "Either you allow me to do the work outside class *or* I'll catch up on my sleep inside class or skip it all together." I needed to rethink the conflict through the lens of mutual interests, reframe the resolution so both parties could get their needs met, and redirect the conflict away from each other. When there is conflict, there is usually some common purpose that unites them. In schools, it is often the common vision, mission, or school improvement goals. When conflict arises, reframe the conflict within the deeper purpose of the work. Individual differences are more easily compromised if both parties can unite on achieving a common goal. Can both parties clearly articulate what they want and how it serves the greater goals? How can both parties get their needs met? In my example, both parties could agree that the most important goal was for Carlos to demonstrate his grasp of the content.

The next thing to consider in conflict is how to make a brave space to have dialogue. This can be accomplished two ways: Communicate authentically that (1) you care about the other party's best interests and (2) you care about them. With Carlos, both parties needed to communicate this to each other. Talking with each party separately, they began to understand the unique challenges the other had. When they came together to dialogue, they were better prepared to express empathy for each other's perspective. Learn how to express care for other people and the interests and challenges they face. You will have a better footing for resolving conflict.

Third, reframe your assumptions. What are you assuming about the other party, and what assumptions are they making about you? Reframe your negative assumptions into a more positive narrative. Mr. Caesar assumed Carlos was too lazy to get out of bed. Carlos assumed Mr. Caesar disliked him and was choosing to prevent him from graduating. Neither assumption was true, but each party needed to conceive an alternative, positive way to juxtapose their relationship. What other reasons might exist for why another person is behaving inappropriately in your view? Can you conceive an alternate truth that might help future dialogues go more smoothly? What questions can you ask that will help you understand the situation or individual better? It is difficult to resolve a problem with a person you fail to understand.

In *Crucial Conversations*, the authors have an approach for speaking persuasively, without being abrasive: Share your facts, Tell your story, Ask for others' paths, Talk tentatively, and Encourage testing.

To redirect conflict, remember our goal of working together collaboratively for the benefit of students. We are not each other's enemies. The real enemies are the things that impede our ability to create a more equitable and inclusive environment for children. Those are the things we want to take down—not each other. When conflicts arise, and they are likely to do so, don't hesitate to point out the enemies of change that have kept us tiptoeing around these mines for years: the fear and ignorance of the atrocities of our complex past, the systems that supported them, and the lack of interpersonal skills to discuss them. Guess what? You can get beyond this because you're learning the skills now.

Postscript: It turns out Mr. Caesar was a young father himself once upon a time. We arrived at an agreed upon arrangement for class attendance and additional tutoring. I had the distinct privilege of handing Carlos his diploma that year and will never forget the grin on his face and the tears in his eyes. He made it! Carlos eventually raised two wonderful educated graduates. And Mr. Caesar? He sacrificially changed the economic trajectory of every member of Carlos's family.

Step 6: Empower for Leadership, Agency, and Activism

You will learn much about yourself in the process, but the ultimate goal is to understand and craft your role in creating a fairer, more equitable, and just system of education for the students in your system or school. It is of little value to spend time cultivating an awareness of injustice if no intentional effort is made to also build personal and collective agency to alleviate it.

Mezirow (2003) argued that the overall purpose of adult development is to realize one's agency through increasingly expanding awareness and critical reflection. As you learn, it is vital to institutionalize the new practices, policies, and procedures by contextualizing the learning, implementing changes, and documenting what is working (Mezirow, 2003).

Contextualized practices anchored in institutionalized or systemic racism, gender marginalization, class discrimination, power imbalances, social inequalities, and other oppressive structures cannot be shrugged off as symptomatic of a society over which we have no control. They can be challenged, confronted, and changed—by you. You are not powerless. At the end of each quarter, reflect on where you are in terms of critical competency, but operationalize your learning with critical action (Freire, 2003). Draft and redraft your school improvement plan and ensure that plan is a living document that reflects the growth you are making as a team together. Craft new policies and rules that institutionalize the behaviors that have demonstrated an ability to promote equity in the environment.

Encourage storytelling of individual journeys, as well as the collective journey of your team, toward greater understanding, agency, and social justice actions. Create reward programs to recognize and honor those who have given their best efforts and energies to implement behaviors and language that promote more equitable opportunities for all. Be fair, accurate, and informative on the specific behaviors that are valued.

When there is a change in leadership, present potential leaders with the documentation of your collective journey and gain agreement that their leadership will not undermine the work that has been undertaken thus far. Share the documentation of your cultural competency journey and improved practices with the superintendent and school board on an annual basis. As you embed new learning, practices, policies, and successes into the culture of the school, you will institutionalize your work, minimalizing the likelihood that the work can be undone with the mere transition of leadership and creating a clear path of succession for future leaders.

Finally, share the work with the people most affected. Racism and oppression rob individuals of their ability to make choices in their best interest, experience the same opportunities as others, or bask in dignity and respect regardless of their surroundings. Activism entails gifting individuals with that which was stolen—their rights, their power, their dignity, and their voice.

Use your voice and your power to ensure everyone has access to the same rights you have always known or were always told were available to you.

Change That Sticks

Planning for conversations on race, culture, and privilege and the dismantling of inequitable systems *before* beginning the change may well limit the surprise factor, unintended sabotage, or perceived resistance when you are navigating this process. Your goal is to (1) navigate successfully through potentially rough waters to achieve your intended goals for students, and (2) use your resources to make changes that are sustainable over time. This can be accomplished if you consider at the outset how you will SCCORE:

- **S**et goals that align with school vision and mission.
- **C**reate a caring community.
- **C**ommunicate with stakeholders.
- **O**rganize for learning.
- **R**ethink, reframe, and redirect conflict.
- **E**mpower for leadership, agency, and activism.

After all, you want the next leader in your building to wander the halls, opening any closet they choose, only to find . . . tangible artifacts of an equitable and inclusive culture.

3

When Silence Abounds: Facilitating Race Discussions Successfully

How do you move a conversation on racial equity forward when someone chooses to avoid it? What can you say when valid questions are met with indifference? What do you do when despite your best efforts, a participant throws up a verbal or nonverbal barrier to communication that fills the space with tension—and the awkward sound of silence?

Talking about race, racism, privilege, power, identity, bias, and micro-aggressions can be a delicate dance. But dancing around the issues rather than through them will confuse the groove, like playing a waltz at a rock concert. To be successful, complex conversations—dialogues that involve a central issue that is analyzed and resolved within the context of multiple competing and interconnected issues—are crucial to routine learning with peers. Complex conversations are a negotiated set of steps that coordinate movement while supporting each individual's growth and expression.

How to successfully navigate a complex conversation, inclusive of topics such as race, is an invaluable skill for culturally competent educators. It's a difficult skill to learn solely within the context of activities, so this chapter is dedicated to building your efficacy to facilitate or participate in difficult conversations that involve race or racism.

Understand That Vulnerability Is Part of the Dance

It's OK to feel vulnerable, insecure, and unsure of your efficacy in conversations of this nature. In fact, it is normal. The likely self-interrogation may begin the moment you observe an injustice. You may ask yourself,

> What am I going to do? Do I know enough to say something? Can a _____ [white, Black, Hispanic, Asian, Native American, and so on—you choose] challenge this without the lived experience of being from another race? Can I challenge a comment or question a policy without looking like I'm a jerk? What if I sound like I don't know what I'm talking about? What if I facilitate this conversation and fail? What do I say if someone calls me a racist?

Smith, Kashubeck-West, Payton, and Adams (2017) refer to this kind of internal scrutiny as *multicultural imposter syndrome*—the discomfort a white instructor may feel when teaching about, facilitating discussions on, or confronting race or racism. You fear that your own biases and racist perspectives may inadvertently surface, and then your intentions may be seen as disingenuous. Or you may feel reluctant to advocate for equity for fear of rejection by peers (Smith et al., 2017). Fear can be paralyzing, and the inclination to remain silent in the face of injustice may feel like the only safe choice. But if you do remain silent, the unintended outcome is likely the perpetuation of injustice. And you're better than that. Your students need your advocacy and your voice.

Sue (2004) underscores the importance of white educator allies as crucial to the movement for educational equity. He notes that it is essential for white educators to mentor, guide, and support other white educators in developing antiracist white identities. Building your cultural competency and unlearning racist ideology is the work of a lifetime. You will experience many moments that will make you want to secretly pump your fist in victory. But you may also experience moments when you make a misstep; phrase something in a way that offends someone; meet with resistance or annoyance; or have your privilege, status, or intellectualism challenged and you secretly want to retreat without speaking another word.

Take heart. Discuss your personal journey of critical consciousness. Seek to understand the critical discourse or experiences that prompted you to reexamine your perceptions. As a learning team, acknowledge and accept internal struggles. Understand there wasn't some magical moment when you flipped a switch and all your biases were zapped out of your subconscious. You may still have a few lingering there. Remind one another that you are human and that we are all in this struggle together for the benefit of the next generation.

So it's OK if you bungle some aspect of this work. Accept a level of anxiety and vulnerability that comes with the territory of complex conversations while resolving to continue to build your professional skills and knowledge. And should you feel like you failed to speak up when you could have, spoke out when you shouldn't have, or failed to demonstrate empathy when presented with a situation that you could not understand, remember that we are continually working through the process of self-discovery and growth. Remind one another of this as many times as you need to. Then fearlessly and courageously continue the conversation.

Embrace and Normalize Discomfort

If you believe it is challenging to help adults learn a foreign language, imagine trying to do so if they were unaware that other languages even existed. Consider how they might respond if they had never seen, heard, or experienced someone speaking another language. Where would you start? Or imagine demonstrating how to effectively wash clothes with a washboard to someone who has always had their clothes professionally laundered? How much enthusiasm might you muster?

For many people, racism is an invisible phenomenon that they have seldom experienced in their own lives. Terminology, such as *privilege* and *micro-aggressions*, may sound strange, complicated, and confusing—practically another language. Modern racism is so hidden within systemic, institutional, structural, and sociocultural practices that it can camouflage its presence; it's a cultural chameleon, transforming just enough to be transparent. It is no wonder that some people question if it is a relic of a bygone era, despite the fact that its insidious existence is current and well documented. Given this context, we are confronted with supporting one another in critical self-reflection that may require the rejection of deeply held values and beliefs, potentially alienating us from people we love and respect. It can be uncomfortable work—deeply uncomfortable.

When people become uncomfortable in an environment, it is normal for them to try to reestablish an environment in which they *do* feel comfortable. Their attempts, however, may result in behaviors that disrupt the equity goals we have committed to achieving. Typical behaviors may include the following (Linder, 2015):

- Becoming defensive.
- Overtly demonstrating disengagement or disinterest.
- Trying to refocus the conversation on another topic.
- Blaming or assigning guilt.
- Assuming intentional personal attacks.
- Displaying resentment, anger, or agitation.
- Refusing to listen to others.
- Behaving disrespectfully.

These behaviors, whether intentional or unintentional, can disrupt productive conversations about race and maintain conditions of inequity without addressing effective ways to dismantle those conditions (Cicetti-Turro, 2007). The tendency to shelter people who identify as white from having discussions or professional development that makes them uncomfortable, even when it's in the best interest of students to do so, is called *white fragility*, a term first coined by DiAngelo (2011). It's defined as "a state in which even a minimum amount of racial stress becomes intolerable, triggering a range of defensive moves . . . such as anger, fear, and guilt, and behaviors such as argumentation, silence, and leaving the stress-inducing situation, [which] function to reinstate white equilibrium" (p. 54).

White teachers can invoke silence with a refusal to cooperate or pleading termination of participation because activities arouse emotions that make them uncomfortable or include beliefs with which they disagree. Often, it can bring the best efforts toward challenging inequitable student outcomes to a screeching halt, followed by an eventual return to maintaining the status quo.

Tatum (1992) framed three sources of resistance to discussing race: (1) the fact that the topic is taboo, (2) the inability of people (mostly white people) to acknowledge racial bias or recognize the influence of racism on their lives, and (3) the socialized belief that the United States is a just society.

Sue (2015) concurs with Tatum (1992) and further theorizes that people who identify as white become uncomfortable talking about race because it challenges their ideologies about how the world works. They have been socialized to believe that racial categorizing has very little to do with anything that happens in life; racism is a product of a bygone era; America is a land of freedom and fairness, and people, regardless of their racial category, generally deserve the treatment they receive. When these ideologies are challenged by counternarratives and stories that tell a different perspective on justice denied, barbaric violence, unmerited aggressions, gross inequities, savage murders, systematic unfairness, and stolen freedom, lands, and dignities, people become defensive, angry, and offended. The messages challenge values they have always believed to be unquestionably true (Sue, 2015). It becomes personal. The message and the messenger challenge the truths of beloved parents, loved ones, and friends. It may give birth to full indignation.

These challenges or barriers to making headway in a conversation about dismantling inequity can feel crippling, but they can be overcome. If these emotions surface, identify how the behaviors might affect the conversation. Are your behaviors impeding or contributing to a productive conversation? Review the goals that you are working toward and focus on them. Then, normalize your discomfort. If you experience discomfort at things you are hearing, information you are reading, or experiences you are having, that is the norm, not the exception. Take a deep breath and lean into it. You are growing, and discomfort is part of the process.

Acknowledge Risks

Discussions about race can feel emotionally, psychologically, and professionally unsafe for people of color, particularly when other members of the group predominately share a different racial identity. DiAngelo and Sensoy (2014) raise the question of whether transformative racial discussions can occur without discursive violence toward people of color. It is not uncommon in racial discussion for white participants to use language to (1) position themselves as completely innocent and unknowledgeable about any kind of racism, (2) position people of color as potentially violent for challenging a dominant perspective or ideology, (3) position themselves as victims of racial discourse, even while speaking with hostility and anger toward others, and/or (4) neutrally position themselves in an idealized nonracial society where race and power live equally (DiAngelo & Sensoy, 2014). These kinds of stances taken in the midst of racial discussions can cause discursive violence toward people of color because it negates the experiences, resources, and evidence that has been shared and reinforces a stereotype of them being violent or angry.

_____

> Thus, the history of extensive, brutal, and explicit physical violence perpetrated by Whites against people of Color—slavery, lynching, whipping, genocide, internment, forced sterilization, and medical experimentation to mention a few—as well as its ideological rationalizations, are trivialized through White claims of a lack of safety when in the rare situation of merely *talking* about race with people of Color. By claiming victimization, Whites obscure the power and privilege we wield and have wielded for centuries. (DiAngelo & Sensoy, 2014, p. 113)

The recommendations for creating a brave space for race conversations acknowledge that any endeavor to do so is for the benefit of *all* parties participating in the discussion. It is ideally not normed for the comfort of one dominant group but rather is intended to support ways that may help everyone feel more comfortable taking the risks of vulnerability and building a nest for authentic dialogue.

First, don't necessarily expect people of color to speak up right away. They may need time and assurance to know there will not be ramifications for thoughts expressed during dialogues that challenge hegemonic social norms. Racial discussions in schools occur within a society where power is imbalanced and white educators hold more of it. Most educators of color are well aware of this dynamic.

Listen empathetically to understand someone else's feelings and perspectives, even if they differ from your own. Everyone has a responsibility to be attentive to their own verbal and nonverbal behaviors as they learn.

Next, *don't ask the singularly few people of color to speak for an entire population of people.* It may feel awkward to be in the minority of a predominately white group of staff members when discussions of race are occurring. Resist the urge to single out the people of color for expertise on all matters concerning children of color. To be clear, educators of color have unique insights concerning the experiences and challenges of being a person of color in a racist society that other teachers may lack. They have shared some of the same types of experiences and challenges as their students of color. But they are not necessarily experts in the sociocultural experiences and challenges of every person of color. You can and should understand each of your students for yourself.

Understanding the cultural beliefs, values, and norms of your students is the work of every teacher. You do not have to be a member of a marginalized group to empathize with the experiences of those who are. Instances of rejection, subjugation, or marginalization are part of the human experience. Any person may have had those experiences within one of their multiple identities (whether they be female, gay, poor, etc.). Help one another make these connections. Become experts together on the cultural norms and values of students, and work cooperatively with parents and the community to do so. Then stick to the norms of making everyone feel included. Although everyone has an opportunity to make a contribution, challenge perspectives such as the ones discussed here that cause discursive violence and prevent transformative discussions and self-reflection. A safe environment is important, but it is well worth your time to define what safety looks like for every participant and which fears are real versus those that are culturally contrived.

Set Norms for Communication

Effective communication "fuels" the culturally competent learning community. Without it, progress grinds to a halt. Nothing about it can be left to chance. Setting norms for how you will talk to one another and agreeing on rules for how you will interact are nonnegotiable. Without these agreements, it only takes one person to derail a discussion; waste time arguing; or interject inappropriate, rude, or insensitive comments that disrupt and discourage other participants. Don't have even the simplest or most innocent conversation about equity without setting norms for how to discuss the topic. If you fail to do so, you may waste precious time trying to clean up an otherwise functional level of positive school culture that someone damaged with a vicious remark.

Here are a few of my favorite norms:

- Every voice is important. Listen respectfully even if you disagree with the message.
- Say whatever you need to say, but do so with kindness.
- Be on time and be prepared.
- Distribute leadership.
- Seek first to understand, then to be understood.

Tatum (2007) used norms to set guidelines for discussing race in her postsecondary classes. Specifically, she asked students to honor the confidentiality of the group. Anyone could ask any question or share a race-related experience without being afraid that their comments or questions would be attributed to them personally when discussing with friends. She discouraged covert put-downs or other derogatory comments that might be used to relieve anxiety or tension during discussions. She also asked students to speak from their own experiences rather than generalizing their experience to others. For example, an appropriate comment might begin as "I think . . ." or "In my experience . . ." (Tatum, 2007).

Once you agree on how you will work and talk together, ensure that the norms are written down, documented, and posted for future meetings. Assign one or more of the team members as *norm keeper*. The role can be rotated. The task of the norm keeper is to signal if or when norms are violated. It can be a simple statement that reminds the participants of the agreed-on rules for communication. Or it can be something fun, like waving a paper flag. If the norms or agreements are violated, focus on them, rather than on the person who violated them. You don't want to silence the offender's voice, but you do want the person to participate in a way that honors the agreements made. Then periodically revisit the norms as a group to ensure that the ones selected are still working effectively or decide whether they need to be modified.

Listen and Speak with Empathy

There is a touching scene in the film *Galaxy Quest* in which the main character, Jason Nesmith, is forced to explain to his alien friend that he is not the commander of an international space station. He is, in fact, merely an actor playing the role of a captain. The alien, Balthazar, looks confused because there is no comparable profession on his planet. Nesmith continues to explain: "I pretended. I lied. On our planet, there are actors who entertain by lying." The alien quivers and moans with emotion. It is inconceivable to him or anyone in his culture that people would deceive others for a living. He has never experienced anything like it.

When people of difference discuss or relay their experiences navigating in a racist society, their comments are often met with a similar sense of disbelief. Those who have never been the target of discrimination, reproof, anger, resentment, or aggression for being different are befuddled and confused by the messages they receive from people who have. There is a tendency to look for reasons to blame the target. What were they doing when the incident occurred? Are they sure they didn't raise their voice or engage in some inappropriate conduct or break the law? Perhaps it was the clothes they were wearing, the car they were driving, or the style of their hair. The listener might even refute the facts and defend the perpetrators. The people, the system, the organization, the government, the institution, or whoever wielded the power to oppress and control could never have actually displayed the behaviors as described, or, if they did, the actions were an innocent oversight; they were never intended to have the outcomes that they did. The fact that someone might be the target of aggression for simply existing is inconceivable to the privileged. They have never experienced anything like it.

To understand the psychological point of view of a group of people who experience the world differently than we do requires the ability to listen and respond without judgment, blame, or negation. It requires empathetic listening and speaking skills.

A number of researchers have demonstrated the empirical utility of empathy for educators (Bilias-Lolis, Gelber, Rispoli, Bray, & Maykel, 2017; Hartman, Johnston, & Hill, 2017; Parsons & Brown, 2001; Warren, 2015, 2018). Empathy is exercised when one individual listens to another for the purpose of understanding that person better. They need not agree with the message being delivered. They are not asked to confirm or negate the validity of the events. They may never have had the same experience as the speaker, even if they were at the same location or event. They do not need to clarify the sequence of events. They do not blame, judge, or interject. They are simply asked to listen and try to understand how another person feels. The role of a seasoned empathetic listener is to begin to make mental connections between the feelings of the speaker and the times in their own lives when they might have felt the same way. They seek to connect with the humanity of another individual, even if they cannot connect with the exact same experience.

This is not easy for most of us to do. From the moment we utter our first string of syllables, we are encouraged to speak. Well before we begin our formal education, we immediately respond when we dissent or disagree. We readily articulate our opinions and perspectives, often asking questions before a speaker is finished. We highly value talking in our culture, and we often take classes in school on public speaking.

But listening? Not so much. I often encourage teams to begin the process of empathetic listening by not responding verbally when the speaker is talking. This can be incredibly difficult, but it's worth the effort after one learns how to relax and listen without having to formulate one's response when the speaker finishes. Practices such as putting yourself into the other person's place, asking open-ended questions after the person has finished talking that encourage them to talk more, and expressing empathy (empathy does not mean agreement) all foster empathetic listening. In time, teams can move into offering appropriate feedback that communicates that the message has been received.

Demonstrating empathy is both an emotional and cognitive skill process (Anderson & Davis, 2012; Batson, Chang, Orr, & Rowland, 2002; Decety et al., 2011). On an emotional level, you are responding with measured restraint, allowing yourself the luxury of listening and learning. On a cognitive level, you are making connections to your own feelings and experiences as you endeavor to accept a perspective different from your own. Learners consistently work to listen without "anticipating, interfering, competing, refuting, or warping meanings into preconceived interpretations" (Johannesen, Valde, & Whedbee, 2013, p. 56). You may never agree with the speaker's perspective, but you can respect their ability to own it, and you can try to understand it.

Define Terms

Ask any gathering of individuals to define *equity*, and you are likely to receive as many answers as there are people. Possible answers may include any of the following:

- Diversity
- Inclusion
- Equality
- Fairness
- Shares issued by a company
- Value in a home
- Rights and responsibilities
- Impartiality
- Social justice
- Making an exception

The trouble with words is that they live in our heads with distinct meanings and definitions as a result of our personal experiences with them. A word could be weighted with meaning, even trauma, for one listener while eliciting no emotion from another listener. To facilitate an effective conversation inclusive of culture, race, or ethnicity, the people engaged in the conversation need to have a common understanding of the key words they are discussing.

This reduces the occurrence of a participant reacting emotionally to a word someone uses without understanding the meaning or intent of the speaker.

Cultural competency, at its core, is a continual process of examining and reevaluating the meaning of events, actions, and one's underlying beliefs. Three questions are always at stake:

1. Are my actions or those of others promoting equity or perpetuating inequity?
2. Am I or others part of the problem or part of the solution to ending racism and privilege?
3. What will I do?

This process of examining and understanding ourselves and the systems in which we operate begins by examining and understanding the words we use and the language we wield to frame critical conversations. Creating meaning together becomes an empowering social process that enables the stakeholders to be an integral part of a mutual construction of meaning rather than the recipient of another's transmission of meaning. Words are powerful receptacles of emotion, and their potency to inflame, negate, or obstruct constructive communication cannot be underestimated (Anderson & Davis, 2012).

Unpacking key vocabulary enables stakeholders to discuss and understand why some words exhume painful emotions or vivid imagery for some colleagues. For example, one staff member joked that he needed someone with white privilege to accompany him into the convenience store so he wouldn't be followed or harassed. Another staff member took immediate offense. The words "white privilege" served as an emotional trigger for him because he misunderstood the meaning of the term or what his colleague was expressing.

One afternoon, the dean of students poked his head into my office and handed me an office referral he had received. I read the referral. "Insubordination. Adam keeps calling me 'Miss.' I have explained to him on several occasions that I am married, but he insists on calling me "Miss." This is deliberately disrespectful behavior." The teacher misunderstood that Adam's salutation was intended as a sign of respect in his culture.

The process of meaning convergence, then, provides for joint possession of common words or cultural vocabulary and lays the groundwork for inclusive participation in learning together, both individually and collectively (Simoes & Esposito, 2014). It is a vital step in helping the community prepare for the work of culturally conscious conversations.

Monitor Language

Be cognizant of the language that you and others use while interacting in small- or whole-group activities. Listen for any language or terms that might marginalize another participant or offend members of the group.

For example, an individual may claim to be colorblind and not see race. That kind of statement implies that simply erasing the racial identity of an individual solves the issue of racism, thereby minimizing the larger issue of institutional and structural racism that maintains oppression of people of color. It also marginalizes the identity of people whose physical features such as hair, skin, and eye color are integral to their identity and of which they are hopefully proud. If someone inadvertently makes a comment that others might find offensive or marginalizing, surface the possibility that the remark could be taken as such and remind all participants of our desire to create a space for dialogue that feels emotionally safe for all members.

Observe Emotions

Observe how your peers are responding emotionally in small or whole groups or in paired activities and dialogues. Be cognizant of body language that suggests anger, frustration, sadness, or pain. Disengagement is not an option, but endeavoring to make some allowance for people who have been through traumatic experiences is permissible. Understand that some staff may have been the target of racial aggression that was emotionally painful. Or they may have been subjected to generational trauma; events that have occurred repeatedly in their family or that were even perpetrated against a family member several generations ago can have detrimental effects on subsequent family members. For example, say that one of your parents or grandparents had been lynched. The effect and trauma of that murder would likely influence the livelihood and experiences of succeeding generations as they recovered from the loss, fear, and horror of that experience.

You might also have someone in the group who may be processing the pain of microaggressions that are occurring on an ongoing basis—the subtle slights and marginalization that happen to people of color every day. As I was sitting in a bakery writing this chapter, a girl of 9 or 10 who looked like she might identify as having Korean ethnicity approached my table and grabbed the chair across from me. I had been elevating my leg on it just moments before. I looked up, raised my eyebrows and met her gaze. She turned and walked away with the chair without uttering a word. I did not shift my gaze as she had done but allowed it to follow her to her table and linger. Her mother approached her and asked, "Mary, did you ask the lady if you could take her chair?" I answered for her lest there be a dispute. "No, she did not, but I would have been happy to do so if she had." I responded. The father approached and stood beside his wife. "What's going on?" he inquired. The wife turned to whisper in his ear, and his face twisted in anger. "Come on everyone," he directed the family. "Let's move someplace else." The family of four picked up their things and reseated themselves on the other side of the restaurant. And that is how the marginalization of people of color and the ideological conditioning that they are to be feared or avoided is passed on generationally. (Do not let the fact that this act was perpetrated by another person of color go unnoticed. People have been socialized to believe there is a hierarchy of status among people of color and those with the darkest skin generally fall at the bottom of that scale.) But that is also the kind of microaggressions that people of color endure on a regular basis.

The term microaggressions was first coined by Chester Pierce about 50 years ago (1970). Microaggressions are brief, subtle, negative or derogatory comments or actions toward people of color that communicate inferiority or hostility toward a person of color (Helms, Nicolas, & Green, 2012; Sue, 2010). They can have a cumulative and devastating effect on one's emotional state (Pierce, Carew, Pierce-Gonzalez, & Willis, 1978). As I tried to return to my writing, the incident kept playing in my head. I pondered how I might have been more instructive to the parents or . . . my thoughts trailed off. Be aware of the emotions of group members, and respond as appropriate to support them while the race conversations occur. One never knows what racial experiences have been resurrected and are playing in their heads.

Create Balance

Self-monitor the amount of time you speak as opposed to the amount of time others speak. Be respectful in providing each participant an opportunity to convey their thoughts without allowing one person to dominate a conversation. Don't forget to invite the person who is silent into the conversation. Ask if they have any thoughts they would like to share, giving every voice respect and equitable opportunity to be heard.

You may have someone who has a favorite topic of interest that they like to steer the conversation toward at any given opportunity. Stay on the topic under discussion and encourage others to do the same. Remind them of the topic and the time allotted to it. If the members of the group express interest in the newly introduced topic, check in to see if they are willing to devote more time to it or if they would prefer to put it to the side to review later on. Most members will appreciate sessions that maintain a clear focus and treat all voices as equals.

Stay Student Centered

Make student outcomes the focus of your work. As educators, our reason for discussions about race is first and foremost about creating more equitable outcomes for all students. Although the work includes understanding the historical and contemporary sociocultural context in which we are educating children and in which we ourselves must work, the goal is to dismantle systems that were created to maintain disparity and to examine and obliterate ways we may be unintentionally perpetuating inequities in the lives of our students. If the conversation gets off track, refocus the dialogue on students. Ask, "What are the implications for students? How do we support the students, given what we have learned? Will the current discussion further our goals of creating more equitable opportunities for students?" If it doesn't, encourage the group to refocus on the topic by examining their work in relation to students.

Get Comfortable with Ambiguity and Accept Nonclosure

The focus of many conversations may be to simply increase understanding. You do not have to solve all the problems that were created before you were born. You cannot eliminate all the obstructions to equity in society. You won't end world hunger in one afternoon. Get comfortable with ambiguity and with the fact that some discussions will end with no clear solution to the issues raised. And that is OK. The dialogue will provide an opportunity for you to better understand the complexity of an issue and the multiplicity of perspectives around it.

Self-Evaluate Your Discussions

Learning to navigate complex conversations requires a support system that provides critical feedback, analysis, and encouragement. Self-evaluate your interactions at the completion of your session. All members can suggest how the next discussion can be improved. Provide peer feedback to one another on basic facilitation or personal interaction skills, and discuss problematic issues that have arisen. Be mindful, however, when discussing interaction issues that you express concerns by focusing on the *problem*, not on a person.

For example, you may choose to discuss the type of behaviors that became an issue and why. Or you might explore the kinds of behaviors that will better support the goals. Reaffirm the importance of listening to and learning from everyone, ensuring that each person understands that they are valued and that you will professionally and objectively handle whatever issues arise as a team.

Build Personal Knowledge

Continue to build your own personal facilitation and personal interaction skills on cultural competency. Read articles, newspapers, and books that provide multiple perspectives on issues of oppression, privilege, power, race, and racism in society. White people, in particular, often fail to see themselves as having a culture. Race discussions often force them to confront the truth of their culture that is inclusive of whiteness and the privileges of whiteness (Glazier, 2003; Helms, 1992). Build personal knowledge about what it means to be white in our society. Explore the benefits of being white, and examine the life outcomes of people who are not. Seek out the voices of people who are different from you and listen to their perspective experiences. Ask yourself how you might feel if you were in their position and find points in their experiences where there is commonality. There are common themes in the human experience—love, fear, hope, and pain, to name a few. Find connections with others. They are there if you look for them.

Use a Conversation Protocol

In the beginning, you may benefit from using a protocol to help organize and focus your discussions. As you become more fluent in having complex conversations, you may develop other strategies for achieving focus and productivity, but the following format should help get you started.

As You Begin
- Review vision/goals/commitments.
- Clarify the purpose, topic, focus, and time commitment.
- Define common terms related to the topic.

- Review norms for communication, and see if any modifications are needed.
- Embrace vulnerability and discomfort. Ask participants if anyone has had an experience with this topic that they would like to share or disclose before you begin.

Getting into the Core of the Work

- Examine data related to the topic, such as student assessments, office referrals, attendance reports, U.S. Department of Education statistics, journal articles, district reports, newspaper articles, or classroom videos.
- Examine systemic and institutional racism. This will involve looking at policies, procedures, and practices related to the topic through an equity lens. Sample questions might include the following:
  - ► What is our written policy on this topic? How well do we follow it?
  - ► What is our vision for equity in our school, and does this particular practice advance it?
  - ► Does the practice in question benefit some and disadvantage others? What are the intentional and unintentional outcomes of the policy? Is the procedure fair and equitable for all of our students?
  - ► Is the practice legally defensible?
  - ► Is there historical context for this practice? Has there been historical precedent for the practice? If so, when and why?
  - ► What is the role of power in this policy? Who has it, who doesn't, and why?
  - ► Were students, parents, and community members integral in establishing the policy? If so, which ones?
  - ► How do we empower all stakeholders to achieve the desired outcome and goals we have set?
  - ► What further learning do we need to achieve the outcomes we have set?
  - ► When, where, and how do we get the additional learning?

Maintaining a Student-Centered Focus

- Summarize the learning, and discuss the implications for students.
- Identify concrete actions and next steps.

Evaluating

- Evaluate the discussion. Were the goals or objectives met?
- What did we do well? What do we need to improve on? What can we celebrate?
- Did the discussion further our goals of creating more equitable opportunities for students? If not, what can we agree to do differently next time?

Move on Despite the Bumps

To move a conversation on racial equity forward, recognize that in order to have a productive conversation, you will have to allow yourself to be vulnerable. You are likely wading into unknown territory for you emotionally, and you may learn some things about yourself that surprise you. Feel free to make mistakes and take risks. It is a journey. Normalize the discomfort you or others may feel in the process, but don't allow anyone to hijack the ride. Your goal is embedded in better student outcomes, and you may need to jealously guard your ride.

Recognize that different people may feel varying levels of risk. Racism has left a bloodied trail of victims in its path that may have been hidden in plain sight from you. Create a brave conversational space where people can speak their truth. And don't underestimate the complexity of the conversation. Multiple barriers are related to the central issue of racism, and you must work to disentangle barriers as you learn how to dismantle them.

Finally, one of the greatest assets you have is one another. As you begin this work together in collaborative learning dialogues and the exercises that follow, you will learn to depend on one another for understanding and support (Buckley & Quaye, 2016). I encourage you to move forward in the direction of the collective vision agreed on despite bumps, barriers, disappointments, mistakes, or glitches that are common in complex conversations. Remember why and for whom you started this work. It's the music that keeps playing in the background as you learn this delicate dance. Don't let anyone silence it. Rather, focus on the far-reaching implications for the next generation in the wake of your success. I didn't say it would be easy, but it definitely is a tango worth the effort.

4

Awaken and Assess

This may feel like one of the scariest things you have ever done professionally. You are commencing a journey that will likely never end and may change the trajectory of your career—most assuredly, positively. By the time we are done, you and your colleagues are going to be better educators, and you will be equipped to manage some of the most complex challenges of our time as they relate to creating equitable learning environments for students.

After today, you may never be the same. The first step is the hardest. You don't quite know what to expect, you may be unsure of what might happen, you may be fearful of conflict, you may be insecure about whom to trust, and you may be hesitant about what to say. Take a deep breath. We'll take it one step at a time, one activity at a time.

The exercises that follow are sequential and build on one another. They are appropriate for educators at any level, including preservice teachers and administrators. Here is the process:

1. **Complete the exercise,** which may or may not include a handout. Note that an activity that might initially appear to be basic in its approach could help promote profound understanding once you have undertaken it with peers and can learn through it together. You can also access the handouts and homework handouts online: www.ascd.org/ASCD/pdf/books/mayfield2020.pdf.

2. **Facilitate discussion.** Each exercise is followed by discussion questions. It is absolutely vital to provide time for rich discussions. Some are more appropriate in partners. In some cases, small-group discussions are recommended, and in others whole-group discussions are suggested. I make this distinction based on the nature of the questions. Questions that are more personal are likely facilitated in pairs or small groups where people can connect more intimately.

3. **Review the key takeaways,** which are brief notes that underscore the intended learning within the exercise. They should not be shared or read prior to completing the exercise or engaging in the discussion.

4. **Assign homework.** Here is where participants can gain background knowledge and additional information that could not be conveyed within the exercise or takeaway notes. The homework assignments are designed to be completed with a learning or thought partner. One should have the same learning partner for at least an entire quarter. It is up to you or your colleagues if you choose to switch each quarter or half the year or remain with the same person throughout the sessions. The assignments are generally designed to be completed outside of the regular time for exercises, although time might be provided for this after the exercises if the community so chooses. In the first activity, when learning partners are selected, I ask them to determine a regular meeting time. Perhaps that is during a planning time at school, after school once a week, or a weekly breakfast, lunch, or happy hour meeting. Cooperatively learning together is a deep part of the commitment of this work and is integral to deepening your learning.

All of the recommended articles are from peer-reviewed journals by deeply regarded scholars or practitioners. They are ideal for learning in both postsecondary and practitioner settings. If you could dedicate the beginning of each new equity meeting to debriefing about the journal articles, this is best. It may bring richer discussion of the topic.

Personal journals are recommended in many of the exercises and can be used to record individual thoughts or reflections. A tablet, notebook, or sheet of paper will work as well. Some will find it interesting to note their thoughts at the beginning of this journey and then at the end. It is one way to compare and reflect on personal growth.

This much you can expect: You will be intellectually challenged, and you will need time to reflect and process your thinking. You will likely feel uncomfortable at times, and you may experience tension. You will disagree with something a colleague says, or they will disagree with you. You will fight for the right words to express yourself professionally. And you may make mistakes. You may want the conversations to cease and may even try to derail them to suit you. It is not uncommon for participants to display anger, dismissiveness, disengagement, intense emotions, disinterest, deliberate ignorance, and defensiveness or engage in deflection or political sabotage. If you see these behaviors, I challenge you at the outset to name any that is disruptive to the process but to continue with the discussion as agreed. If you persist with resolve and resilience, your efforts will be rewarded.

Here is what you can expect on the other side of these conversations: You will learn some history and facts that were deliberately excluded from your formal schooling curriculum. You will be able to recognize the far-reaching tentacles of racial bias and oppression hidden in plain sight. You will understand yourself, your students, and other people with different cultural values better. You will recognize the role of privilege and power in our society and be able to identify its presence in most environments. You will know some of the most destructive kinds of racism and how to dismantle systems that demonstrate them. You will look to the future with hope because you will have the tools to create it. You will be a better educator with skills that can be rendered in global environments and multiple cultures. You will begin a process of transformation. Have the courage to not allow anyone to derail that.

Exercises for Quarter 1

Following are 21 exercises that you may pick and choose among as you *awaken* to the urgency of confronting racial bias and you learn to *assess* its pervasiveness in individuals and systems. This will be the focus of our work during this first quarter of the school year.

Exercise 1: Musical Pairs

Time: 12 minutes

Materials: Large room with space for movement; music player

Learning Objective: To select a homework learning partner for the quarter

Facilitator Guidelines:

1. Ask participants to form two concentric circles. The outer circle should face inward, and the inward circle should face outward. Ultimately, each participant should be facing another participant.

2. Turn on some music. Direct the outward circle to step to the right until you stop the music. The inward circle remains static.

3. Turn the music back on. Then direct the inward circle to step to the left, until you stop the music.

4. Announce, "When the music ceases, the person standing in front of you is your homework learning partner for the quarter. Introduce yourselves if they are unknown to you." [Pause for a minute, if appropriate.]

5. Say, "Now partners, you need to look one another in the eye, raise your right hands, and repeat after me: 'I solemnly promise to be the best learning partner I can be, in rain or in shine, to learn and to grow from this day forward, for better, for worse, when I agree, and when I disagree. I will keep your confidences and strive to maintain your trust. You can depend on me.'"

6. Say, "By the power invested in me, you are now officially homework learning partners for this quarter. At the end of the quarter, you must come to a mutual decision to select another partner or remain together."

7. Say, "There is an expectation that you will meet with this person once a week."

8. Say, "As a symbol of your commitment to this process this year, each of you will receive a personal journal to document your questions, reflections, and growth. [Pass out journals.] Congratulations! You may shake your partner's hand!"

Homework: Exchange information about common planning times, or set up a standard time to meet for breakfast, lunch, coffee, happy hour, or some mutually agreeable time for discussion during the week.

Exercise 2: Personal Mission Statement

Time: 25 minutes

Materials: Colored pencils, markers, or crayons and individual sheets of paper for each participant; Exercise 2 handout

Learning Objective: To determine your personal mission statement

Facilitator Guidelines:

1. Ask participants to draw a picture of their future selves as they have always dreamed of being or as doing something they have always hoped to accomplish professionally.

2. Ask participants to list their three greatest talents or gifts on the right side of the picture.

3. Ask them to list three things or causes they feel strongly about on the left side of the picture.

4. Underneath the picture, they should list three professional accomplishments they are most proud of achieving thus far. They have 15 minutes to complete this activity.

5. At the end of the allotted time, each participant should find a partner and explain their drawing to them.

Homework: Write your personal mission statement. The Exercise 2 handout offers some examples. Before the next meeting, meet with your learning partner to share and discuss your personal mission statements. Together you may choose to refine or modify them. Hold onto them because you will need to bring them to your next meeting. (The statements are not secret. When complete, please post them in the staff lounge to share with your colleagues.)

Exercise 2 Handout: Examples of Personal Mission Statements

What is a mission statement? It can

- Be a statement that establishes what is important to you.
- Define who you are, how you will live, and what gives purpose or meaning to your life.
- Be a self-imposed duty or task you feel called to perform.
- Be short and concise enough for you to remember and articulate easily.
- Be a framework for how you want to live your life.
- Create boundaries for what you will or won't accept in your life.

Questions to Ask Yourself

- What are you passionate about?
- What do you do better than anyone else?
- What energizes you?
- What do you value?
- What inspires you?
- What makes you great?

Examples of Personal Mission Statements

- My mission is to serve others through leadership, inspire others through my creativity, and encourage others with extraordinary kindness.
- My mission is to experience a sense of wonder, adventure, and accomplishment every day and inspire it in all who meet me.
- My mission is to enjoy the beauty of the natural environment and teach others to treat our planet with compassion and care.
- My mission is to communicate the love of God to my family, friends, and neighbors, known and unknown.
- My mission is to use my gifts of enthusiasm, intelligence, and organization to help others organize their spaces and live more productive lives.

What is your personal mission statement? What is your purpose?

_____

_____

_____

_____

_____

Exercise 3: Write Down to the Core

Time: 20 minutes

Materials: One item participants bring that represents one of their core values; participant mission statements from Exercise 2; Exercise 3 handout, filled out previously by each participant

Learning Objective: To identify one's core values

Facilitator Guidelines:

1. Distribute the Exercise 3 handout one week before the meeting. It asks participants to identify an item that represents one of their core values, bring it to the next meeting, and be prepared to share it in small groups.

2. Ask participants to divide into groups of three to four. (Note: Anything larger will likely not allow time for everyone to participate.) In small groups, members of the group each write down a core value they believe another member of the group possesses, based on their observations of that person. Allow time for participants to complete before proceeding.

3. Participants then describe the item they brought, explain why it represents one of their core values, and reveal the other core values they identified for themselves in the handout. They should also discuss how that core value manifests in their personal or professional lives.

4. Now the other members of the group have a chance to reveal the core value they chose for that participant and explain why they chose it. This continues until all members of the group have had a chance to share and receive feedback on their observed core value.

Small-Group Debrief:

- What core values did you have in common with other members of your group?
- What core values were unique only to you?
- How might you use your core values to fulfill your personal mission?

Whole-Group Debrief:

- Is it fair to associate some core values with an ethnic culture or racial category? What is the relationship between values and race, if any? Give an example of a racial stereotype linked to a core value. Why might some people make that association?

Exercise 3 Handout: Write Down to the Core

Personal core values are

- Principles that highlight what you stand for.
- Things that are important to you.
- Ideologies that clarify who you are.
- Strongly held beliefs about what is acceptable.
- Things you choose to exhibit in your life.
- Decision guidelines that keep you true to yourself.

Questions to Ask Yourself

- Who are your heroes, and what traits do they possess?
- What would you defend to keep?
- What is more important to you than anything else in the world?
- What characteristics do you hope others see in you?
- What trait do you expect in role models?
- What traits or characteristics do you admire in others?
- What standards of behaviors do you uphold?

Examples of Personal Core Values

- Acceptance, exploration, professionalism, fairness, reason, balance, generosity, calm, self-reliance, happiness
- Imagination, joy, kindness, teamwork, leadership, dedication, meaning, openness, unity, originality, family
- Effectiveness, passion, vision, wealth, accountability, accomplishment, brilliance, acceptance, ambition, independence
- Adaptability, bravery, creation, accuracy, amusement, energy, alertness, integrity, achievement, intelligence
- Comfort, strength, freedom, spirituality, creativity, courage, order, enjoyment, health, awareness

List your core values, then bring one item that represents one of them to the next meeting.

_____

_____

_____

_____

Exercise 4: Culture Club, Part A

Time: 15 minutes

Materials: Exercise 4 handout, Exercise 4 homework handout (see p. 189)

Learning Objective: To examine beliefs and values we learned in our family culture

Facilitator Guidelines:

1. At your signal, have participants organize into pairs. Pass out the Exercise 4 handout.

2. Ask participants to select three questions about their family cultural values and beliefs they are comfortable discussing with their partner. Each person has six minutes.

3. At the six-minute mark, ask pairs to switch speakers so the other person also has six minutes to share.

Small-Group Debrief:

- What biases, if any, did you hear as you or your partner spoke? They can be quite innocent, such as a preference for large families versus small.
- How might those biases surface in the learning environment?

Whole-Group Debrief:

- What surprised you?
- Which cultural values did you share with your partner? Which ones did you not share?
- What are the values and beliefs of your students' cultures?

Homework: Read "Culture, Literacy, and Power in Family–Community–School–Relationships" by Concha Delgado Gaitan (2012). Discuss with your learning partner using the questions in the Exercise 4 homework handout.

Exercise 4 Handout: Learning Partner Discussion Questions

You learn beliefs and values from your cultural influences. Today you will have an opportunity to discuss them with a partner. Read all the questions first and decide which ones you would like to discuss. You may choose to focus on only one or two topics. Be flexible. Be you. There is no mandate that you discuss every question. Meaningful discussion is prized above covering the topics. You have 12 minutes to discuss with 6 minutes for each partner.

Your Family Values and Beliefs

1. Family: What constitutes a family? What was your family structure like? What is the role of families?

2. Language: What language was spoken in your home? How did people communicate with one another? How many people spoke more than one language? What beliefs about language were shared?

3. Religion: How important was religion in your home? How was it discussed or observed? How do these messages influence you today, if at all?

4. Education: How was your family involved in your education? What expectations were communicated about education? Who served as the greatest influence for you in choosing your current career?

Exercise 5: My Town, Part A

Time: 15 minutes

Materials: Personal journals or a sheet of paper

Learning Objective: To discuss how our cultural environment influenced values and beliefs

Facilitator Guidelines:

1. Ask participants to write down the first three words that come to mind when they think of the community they most consider their "hometown" (3 minutes).

2. Ask participants, in groups of three, to share the words they wrote down and why they selected those words. (3 minutes)

3. Next, have participants discuss how their community influenced their current values and beliefs.

Whole-Group Debrief:

- What values or beliefs did you learn in your community? Write down three answers to serve as Venn Diagram Circle 1 and stash it in your personal journal for later.

- In what ways, do you believe, is the community influencing the beliefs and values of your students?

Key Takeaway: Our community and culture influence our values and beliefs.

Exercise 6: My Town, Part B

Time: 15 minutes

Materials: Personal journals or a sheet of paper

Learning Objective: To discuss how our cultural environment influenced values and beliefs

Facilitator Guidelines:

1. Ask participants to write down the first three words that come to mind when they think of the community in which they are currently working. (3 minutes)

2. Ask participants, in groups of three, to share the words they wrote down and why they selected those words. (3 minutes)

3. Have each participant discuss what they believe are the current values and beliefs of the community in which they work.

Whole-Group Debrief: What do you believe are the values or beliefs in this school's community? Write down three answers to serve as Venn Diagram Circle 2 and stash it in your personal journal for later.

Key Takeaway: Every community has values and beliefs.

Exercise 7: My Town Reality Check, Part A

Time: 25 minutes

Materials: Exercise 7 handout

Learning Objective: To discuss how our cultural environment influenced values and beliefs

Facilitator Guidelines:

1. In advance of this meeting, invite no fewer than three parents or community members to discuss their community's values and beliefs. Provide them with the five questions listed in rounds 1–5 below.

2. Pass out the Exercise 7 handout, and ask participants to respond to questions in the lower right circle before you begin. When complete, introduce the panel of parents/community members. In five rounds of questioning, have each participant answer the following questions:

   ▸ Round 1: What three words might you use to describe this community, and why?

   ▸ Round 2: Name three things you value, and why.

   ▸ Round 3: What dreams and hopes do you have for your child/grandchild/stepchild/student?

   ▸ Round 4: What barriers does your child/grandchild/stepchild face?

   ▸ Round 5: If you had the opportunity to teach this staff one thing, what would it be?

   ▸ Wrap-Up: Thank the panel.

Whole-Group Debrief: Complete the Venn diagram in the Exercise 7 handout. Use the information from the Venn Diagram circles 1–3 to analyze the following questions:

- Which values intersected in your diagram?
- What surprised you?
- What did you learn?
- Which values do you have in common with the people in this community?

- Which values did you predict this community had that were confirmed by community members? Which values were not?
- How can you use what you learned in your relationships with students and parents?

Key Takeaways:

- Some of the community values and beliefs you learned are also taught in this school community.
- Before assuming you understand the values and beliefs in a community in which you do not live, ask the people who live there.
- We can all learn something from everyone.

Follow Up: If appropriate, arrange for the parent and community members to sign up to conduct Lunch and Learns, presenting the one topic they suggested they would like to teach to staff members.

Exercise 7 Handout: Venn Diagram

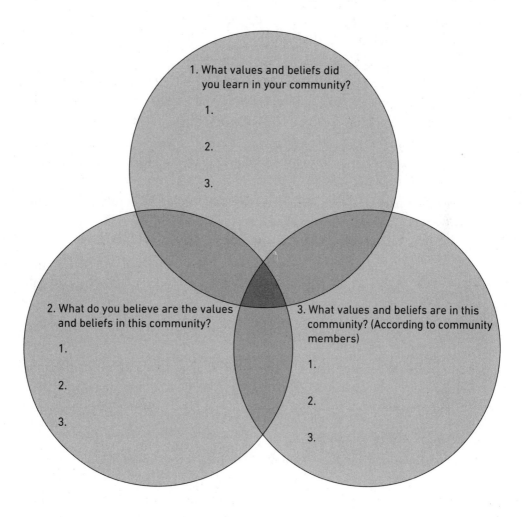

1. What values and beliefs did you learn in your community?

   1.

   2.

   3.

2. What do you believe are the values and beliefs in this community?

   1.

   2.

   3.

3. What values and beliefs are in this community? (According to community members)

   1.

   2.

   3.

Exercise 8: Identity Meetup, Part A

Time: 20 minutes

Materials: Personal journals

Learning Objective: To unpack our personal identities as individuals and the influences that shaped them

Facilitator Guidelines:

1. Tell participants they have three minutes to write down in their journals five words or phrases that describe their identity as an individual (e.g., honest, white, short, opinionated, mother).

2. At your signal, have them organize into groups of three to four. (Note: If groups are larger than this, it is likely someone will not have an opportunity to share.)

3. Ask participants to unpack the following questions in their small groups. Each question has an assigned time of approximately three minutes.

   ▸ Share and discuss how you defined yourself.

   ▸ What people or experiences have informed your identity descriptors?

   ▸ Did a teacher influence your identity, positively or negatively? What did they say or do?

   ▸ How can teachers help students construct positive identities of themselves?

   ▸ What can you do tomorrow to support students' positive identity construction? Document the proposed options and revisit them next quarter.

Whole-Group Debrief:

- How does your identity or what you believe about yourself influence your behavior?

- What ideas did you discuss for how to help students construct a positive identity?

Key Takeaways:

- A positive self-identity increases a person's sense of worth, belonging, and emotional well-being.

- As educators, we can have a powerful influence on a student's self-identity.

Exercise 9: Jingle All the Way

Time: 25 minutes

Materials: Exercise 9 handout

Learning Objective: To understand how media messages influence bias within our culture

Facilitator Guidelines: Pass out the Exercise 9 handout, and ask participants to complete the popular slogans and jingles.

Whole-Group Debrief:

- How many jingles or slogans were you able to recall?
- Why were you able to recall a jingle or slogan that likely had no personal significance for you?
- What sayings or quotations do you cite that students might associate with you?

Key Takeaways:

- Media messages are intended to influence. We receive and store them in our subconscious all the time.
- The messages can sometimes contain biases or reinforce stereotypes that we also receive, store in our subconscious, and recall without scrutinizing their messaging. Examples include
  - ▸ A popular fashion retailer that advertises a Black child wearing a sweatshirt labeling him a monkey.
  - ▸ A beer manufacturer that runs an advertisement in which a beer mug slides down a bar passing numerous people with dark skin but stops in front of a woman with light skin before flashing the message that sometimes "lighter is better."
  - ▸ Television programs that routinely show Black men in handcuffs and white men in suits or uniforms.
  - ▸ News programs that display pictures of well-dressed and smiling people with light skin while showing people with darker skin disheveled and menacing—even when the alleged perpetrator has light skin.
  - ▸ Movies or television shows staged in urban cities that lack ethnically, culturally, physically, or racially diverse characters.
- Most jingles and slogans may be harmless, but messages that subtly convey superiority of one group of people over another shape the way we perceive others and ultimately how we interact with them.

Homework: Look for subtle messages of bias in television shows, news reports, and print media. Share your best examples with your learning partner.

Exercise 9 Handout: Jingle All the Way

Finish these popular advertising jingles and slogans:

1. Gimme a break, gimme a break, _____.
2. The best part of waking up _____.
3. Plop, plop, fizz, fizz _____.
4. Like a good neighbor, _____.
5. Meow, meow, meow, meow, _____.
6. My bologna has a first name, _____.
7. Melts in your mouth, _____.
8. The quilted quicker _____.
9. The few. The proud. _____.
10. Every kiss begins with _____.
11. You're in good hands _____.
12. Fifteen minutes can save you _____.

Exercise 10: Uno, Dos, Tres!

Time: 20 minutes

Materials: A deck of Uno cards for each small group (you may have any-where from 2–10 people in a group); a room with tables and chairs for participants; Exercise 10 homework handout (see p. 190)

Learning Objective: To explore the value of and prejudices concerning multilingualism

Facilitator Guidelines:

1. Have participants seat themselves at a table. Distribute a deck of Uno cards to each group.

2. Explain the rules of the game—that each player is dealt seven cards; that there is a draw pile and a discard pile; that the object of the game is to play all the cards in your hand; and that players do so by matching a card in their hand with the number, color, or symbol/action of the card displayed in the discard pile. If players require further instruction, they can check out the rules online.

3. Stop the game after 10 minutes or after a group has declared a winner.

Whole-Group Debrief:

• Think of this game as a metaphor for multiple language acquisition and retention.

• Imagine each of the four different colors of the cards represented a different language you were capable of speaking.

• Discarding your card was your opportunity to use the language in your possession.

• However, your ability to use your language was greatly influenced by other members in the group. They could play action cards that served as barriers and limited your ability to play the cards in your possession.

• Thank goodness for the wild card—the person, place, or thing that recognized your value and allowed you to play in a way that helped you be more successful.

• In your groups, discuss any analogies or lessons you might draw from this metaphor about multilingualism after playing this game. After five minutes, ask people to share key points from their discussions.

Whole-Group Discussion:

• Why don't we place a higher value on bilingualism and multilingualism in our culture?

• How can we reinforce the value of multilingualism among our students?

Key Takeaways:
- The ability to speak more than one language is an asset.
- Language connects you with your heritage, history, and family.
- Bilingualism provides more work opportunities globally.
- Please don't be the person who puts up barriers for people when they try to use their language assets.
- Be a wild card. Foster the successful acquisition, retention, and proficiency of all languages.

Homework: Read "Rethinking Bilingual Instruction" by Patricia Gándara (2015). Discuss with your learning partner using the questions in the Exercise 10 homework handout.

Exercise 11: Picture This

Time: 25 minutes

Materials: Exercise 11 handout, Exercise 11 homework handout (see p. 191)

Learning Objective: To introduce the construction of race

Facilitator Guidelines:

1. Pass out the Exercise 11 handout and ask participants to complete it. Tell them they have five minutes.
2. After three minutes, inform participants that the category rules have changed. They must correct their errors based on new rules. The new categories are White, Black, Mulatto or Mixed Race, Black Slave, Mulatto Slave, and Indian. They have one minute to recategorize the people.
3. After one minute, inform participants that the category rules have changed. They must correct their errors based on the new rules. The new categories are White, Black, Indian, Chinese, and Japanese. They have one minute to recategorize the people.
4. After one minute, inform participants that the category rules have changed. They must correct their errors based on the new rules. The new categories are White, Black, Aleut, Eskimo, American Indian, Chinese, Japanese, Filipino, Hawaiian, and Part-Hawaiian. They have one minute to recategorize the people.
5. After one minute, inform participants that the category rules have changed. They must correct their errors based on the new rules. The new categories are White, Black, Another Race, Chinese, Japanese, Filipino, Korean, Asian, Vietnamese, Other Asian, Native Hawaiian, Samoan, Guamanian, Other Pacific Islanders, Mexican, Puerto Rican, Cuban or other Hispanic, Latino, Spanish. They have one minute to recategorize the people.

Whole-Group Debrief:

- Why is it difficult to categorize people by race or ethnicity?
- Why do we categorize people this way?
- How are we using those labels in our conversations with students, parents, or the community?
- How do we use those labels in our heads?

Key Takeaways:

- When the U.S. Census Bureau began categorizing people in 1790, there were only three categories: Free and White, All Other Free People, and Slaves. These categories set the groundwork for establishing racial categories based on who had the power and opportunity to pursue life, liberty, and the pursuit of happiness—and who did not.
- The categories shifted over time, constructed by societal attitudes, economics, and politics.
- Up until 1960, census-takers determined for themselves the race of the people they counted—a veritable guessing game.
- When used as a descriptor for categorizing people, race is an inefficient, unreliable, and fluid guessing game in which society changes the rules to suit its needs.
- Far too often, you cannot tell the race of someone simply by looking at them.
- Racial categories have historically served as a code for categorizing those granted power, privileges, and influence and those who typically have not been granted these things. Historically, people of color have been categorically denied power and socioeconomic privileges.

Homework: Complete Exercise 11 homework handout. Note: If you would like to print out color copies of this handout, go to www.ascd.org/ASCD/pdf/books/mayfield2020.pdf.

Exercise 11 Handout: Picture This

Place the people below in one of the following categories:

1. Free White People (does not include Irish, Jewish, or Italian)
2. All Other Free People
3. Slaves

Please use a pencil. This could get messy.

_____ _____ _____ _____

_____ _____ _____ _____

Exercise 12: Culture Club, Part B

Time: 15 minutes

Materials: None

Learning Objective: To examine beliefs and values we learned in our family culture

Facilitator Guidelines:

1. At your signal, have participants organize into pairs. (Note: If groups are larger than this, it is likely someone will not have an opportunity to share.)

2. Ask participants to select three areas of their family cultural values and beliefs, past or present, from the list below. Next, they should fill out the Exercise 12 handout. They may choose to refer to this information later in Exercise 26. Each person has five minutes to share their thoughts on the three areas they selected.

3. At the five-minute point, ask pairs to switch speakers so both people have five minutes to share their ideas about their three selections.

Family Cultural Values:

- Personal space
- Traditional foods
- Acceptable and unacceptable dress
- Traditions and histories that are a source of pride

Whole-Group Debrief:

- What surprised you?
- Which cultural values did you share with your partner? Which ones did you not share?
- What biases did you hear as you or your partner spoke?
- How might those biases surface in the learning environment?

Exercise 12 Handout: Beliefs and Values Learned in Your Culture

- What foods are traditionally served at your family gatherings?

  _____

  _____

  _____

  _____

- How do people in your family typically dress? What is acceptable, and what is not?

  _____

  _____

  _____

  _____

- What are the histories, traditions, and holidays that are a source of pride in your family?

  _____

  _____

  _____

  _____

- What topics are not discussed openly?

  _____

  _____

  _____

  _____

Exercise 13: My Town Reality Check, Part B

Time: 25 minutes

Materials: Personal journals

Learning Objective: To discuss how our cultural environment influenced values and beliefs

Facilitator Guidelines:

1. Ahead of time, invite no fewer than three students to discuss their community's values and beliefs. Provide them with the five questions below.

2. Introduce the panel of students. In five rounds of questioning, have each student answer the following questions:

   ▸ Round 1: What three words might you use to describe your neighborhood, and why?

   ▸ Round 2: Name three things you value, and why.

   ▸ Round 3: What dreams/hopes do you have?

   ▸ Round 4: What barriers do you feel you face?

   ▸ Round 5: If you had the opportunity to teach this staff one thing, what would it be, and why?

   ▸ Wrap-up: Thank the student panel.

Whole-Group Debrief: Facilitate a group discussion using the following questions:

- What surprised you?
- What did you learn?
- Which values do you share with the students on the panel?
- Which values, if any, were discussed by students but were not addressed by community members interviewed earlier?
- How can you use what you learned in your relationships with students and parents?

Key Takeaway: Many of your community values and beliefs are similar to the ones in this community.

Follow-Up: If appropriate, arrange for the students to sign up to conduct Lunch and Learns, presenting the one topic they suggested they would like to teach to staff members.

Exercise 14: Identity Meetup, Part B

Time: 20 minutes

Materials: Personal journals

Learning Objective: To unpack how we internalize positive and negative messages about ourselves

Facilitator Guidelines: In Exercise 8, participants chose words that described their identity or how they saw themselves.

1. Tell participants they have one minute to review the words or phrases they used to describe themselves in Exercise 8 (which they wrote down previously in their journals). They can modify those words now if they choose.

2. At your signal, have the participants organize into pairs. (Note: If groupings are larger than this, it is likely someone will not have an opportunity to share).

3. Ask participants to unpack the following questions. Each question has an assigned discussion time of five minutes.

   ▸ Take turns reading one of the five words or phrases you chose to describe yourself. Discuss the positive and negative messages you have heard about each of the descriptors. For example, what are some positive and negative messages you have seen or heard about being short?

   ▸ How do you create emotional safety, equitable treatment, and positive identity development when you have some students who belong to groups where the messages seen and heard are largely positive and other students who belong to groups where the messages seen and heard are largely negative?

   ▸ How do you reduce bias and create equitable opportunities when you have some staff members who belong to groups where the messages seen and heard are largely positive and other staff members who belong to groups where the messages seen and heard are largely negative?

Whole-Group Debrief:

• How would we recognize students who have internalized messages of superiority? What might we see or hear?

• How would we recognize students who have internalized messages of inferiority? What might we see or hear?

• What can we do?

Exercise 15: Benefits and Barriers

Time: 60 minutes (This session is given more time because of the complexity of the topic.)

Materials: Personal journals

Learning Objective: To discuss how our racial identity has influenced our lives

Facilitator Guidelines:

1. Have participants read "White Privilege: Unpacking the Invisible Knapsack" by Peggy McIntosh (1989).

2. Ask them to self-reflect on the reading by writing a short paragraph about themselves in their journals that they won't mind sharing, using the following prompts:

    ▸ Which privileges outlined in the article have you personally experienced?

    ▸ What other benefits and privileges have you enjoyed in your lifetime?

    ▸ What barriers have you faced in your lifetime?

    ▸ Which benefits or barriers might you attribute to your racial identity?

    ▸ Why are many of the lived experiences of people with white skin different from the lived experiences of people with dark skin?

    ▸ What ways can racism exist outside of individual interactions?

3. After five minutes, ask participants to swap paragraphs with a nearby partner. Each partner has two uninterrupted minutes to discuss their reflection on their partner's paragraph. The conversation that ensues should incorporate empathetic speaking and listening skills. Here are some useful prompts:

    ▸ Tell me more about . . .

    ▸ I'm not sure what you meant by . . . Can you explain more?

    ▸ Why do you see that as a benefit?

    ▸ Why do you see that as a barrier?

    ▸ Help me understand how you formed your thinking.

    ▸ Can you help me understand . . . ?

    ▸ I appreciate you explaining your thinking.

    ▸ If that happened to me, I might feel the same way.

Whole-Group Debrief:

• What surprised you?

• What ways can racism exist outside of individual interactions?

• Benefits experienced as a result of your race are termed *privileges*. Why do you think some people reject that term?

Key Takeaways:

- Privilege has nothing to do with hard work. One can work hard and still not be extended certain privileges (e.g., the ability to be listened to or trusted) that others are granted without question. There are social, emotional, psychological, and economic privileges extended to people who own white skin.

- An example of racism is when a group of people benefit from privileges and power at another group of people's expense.

- Racism is more than individual interactions. Racism can be leveraged by systems and institutions. Systems and institutions can and have granted privileges to some based on the color of their skin.

Exercise 16: Get Out of Jail Free Card

Time: 35 minutes
Materials: Exercise 16 handout, Exercise 16 homework handout (see p. 192)
Learning Objective: To understand the role of racial categories
Facilitator Guidelines:

1. Ask the staff to divide into groups of four to five, then pass out the Exercise 16 handout with the "Get Out of Jail Free Card" scenario for participants to read.

2. After five minutes, ask each team to present their defense to the whole group. Allow no more than five minutes per team. After presentations, the whole group votes for the team with the "best defense" and deserving of a Get Out of Jail Free Card.

Whole-Group Debrief: Which groups, if any, chose to blame the murder victims in some way? Why?

Key Takeaways:

- Blaming victims of violence for the violence perpetrated on them has a long history. Colonialism, which included kidnapping, murder, assault, forced entry, and armed robbery of the property and possessions of rightful owners, was justified by elaborately crafted narratives. These narratives portrayed the victims as savage, incapable, inept, ignorant, animalistic, inferior, and overall deserving of the treatment they received.

- Racial categories were a simplistic way to assign power, economic status, and other privileges to people. In the same way that your group was careful to craft the language to justify your crimes, colonizers were careful to craft the language that was assigned to racial categories. Whites were characterized as intelligent, Christian, hard-working, sexually demure, trustworthy, and innocently seeking to establish a fair democracy and capitalism, yet victims of others' aggressive natures. People of color were characterized as less intelligent, savage, lazy, criminally inclined, physically strong, sexually aggressive, sneaky, not to be trusted, and lost without the guidance and direction of white people.

- Crimes that would normally have been fiercely prosecuted and punished were met with leniency or indifference because the narratives were accepted and the ideology took root that some people deserved much, whereas others deserved much less. Owning white skin came with power and privileges that were fiercely protected.

- The systematic rape, pillage, theft, and murder perpetrated on people in certain racial categories gave some people a Get Out of Jail Free Card, while simultaneously throwing others into generational psychological, social, and economic imprisonment.

- Racial categories, when examined closely, align with levels of power, status, and influence. People of color with higher levels of power, status, and influence are more likely subject to having it revoked at any time and for any reason.

Homework: Read "Embodying Decoloniality: Indigenizing Curriculum and Pedagogy" by Karlee D. Fellner (2018). Discuss with your learning partner using the questions in the Exercise 16 homework handout.

Exercise 16 Handout: "Get Out of Jail Free Card" Scenario

You and your colleagues, hereby known as (the defendants), may possibly be charged with the following crimes:

- Unlawful entry
- Kidnapping
- Armed robbery
- Assault with a deadly weapon
- Murder, first degree
- Fraud

Truth is, you and the other defendants knowingly committed each of the crimes above. In fact, on the night in question, the local police found you and the other defendants in the home of the murder victims with blood splattered clothes. There was clear evidence of forced entry and a crowbar in your handbag. Your fingerprints and those of the other defendants were found throughout the home and on the murder weapons. There had been a botched attempt to conceal the bodies in the backyard, but they were located in shallow graves and a shovel was found in your trunk. Your next-door neighbor's stolen vehicle was parked in the driveway of the crime scene, and your bloodied fingerprints are on the steering wheel. DNA analysis confirms the blood on your clothes and the wheel match the victims. *It doesn't look good.*

However, the judge is known to be fair and lenient. If you and your colleagues can contrive a convincing explanation, you could walk out a free person. It's happened before. Work collaboratively with your colleagues to design the most convincing defense possible that justifies your actions on the night of said event—oh, and you only have five minutes before the preliminary hearing begins.

Exercise 17: Categories

Time: 60 minutes

Materials: A stack of index cards with stereotype labels (see Exercise 17 handout); a large room with space (this exercise involves a lot of movement); Exercise 17 homework handout (see p. 193)

Learning Objective: To understand common assumptions about race and personality traits

Facilitator Guidelines:

1. Say, "I'm going to ask you to categorize yourself into the corner that you believe best matches your physical traits. Once you are in the corner, each group selects a group facilitator who will be given some cards with characteristics. As the group facilitator reads off the characteristics, check if everyone in your group has the same characteristics." [As the facilitator in charge of the activity, you will be moving quickly to distribute, shuffle, and redistribute the cards to each group in each round. Wear comfortable shoes.]

2. Commence Round 1, Hair color: Blondes go to corner 1, brunettes go to corner 2, redheads go to corner 3, and those with gray hair or who are bald go to corner 4. When participants arrive at their corners, have the facilitator for each group read a list of characteristics to see if everyone in the group fits the characteristic. After three minutes, ask the groups if they were successful in identifying a characteristic that every individual in the group shared. Heads up: It is far from likely. Collect the cards, reshuffle, and do a second round.

3. Commence Round 2, Eye color: Those with blue eyes go to corner 1, those with brown eyes go to corner 2, those with green eyes go to corner 3, those with gray eyes go to corner 4, and those with hazel eyes go to middle of room. When participants arrive at their designated spots, have the facilitator for each group read a list of characteristics to see if everyone in the group fits the characteristic. After three minutes, ask the groups if they were successful in identifying a characteristic that every individual in the group shared. Heads up: It's far from likely.

4. Ask participants to be seated for the debrief.

Partner Share:

- What are some racial stereotypes you have seen or heard in schools?
- If you challenged the stereotypes when you heard them, discuss with your partner what you said or did.

If you failed to challenge the stereotype when you heard it, discuss why you chose not to. What did you fear? Did the fear include the revocation of social acceptance, status, power, or influence? Is that real?

Whole-Group Debrief:

- Why do some people presume that people who share the same physical characteristics, such as skin color, share common personality or character traits? Where did that logic come from?

- How might that kind of thinking affect one's work with students? Parents? Community members? Staff?

- What might that look like when students internalize negative stereotypes about themselves?

Key Takeaways:

- When the United States was being established, colonizers were met with some difficult challenges: (1) There was a great deal of work that needed to be done to build an empire; and (2) the European immigrants did not speak the same language as the indigenous people who occupied much of the land. So a decision was made to take the land by force and coerce other people to do all the work. To do that with moral impunity, narratives were contrived. Native Americans were demonized as savage or ignorant, and Africans were dehumanized as primitive or violent. These kinds of labels and narratives made it easier to justify the inhumane enslavement of humans, murder, pillage, destruction of communities, and theft of tribal lands.

- Fast-forward to now. Some of these same narratives linger within our psyche, passed down from generation to generation and from culture to culture. The narratives remain within our ways of acculturation in terms of generalized messages about people and categorizations of people based on the color of their skin.

- Melanin, a structural formulation of cells that determines skin and eye color, does not determine personality or character traits. But the negative narratives contrived about particular groups of people suggest that it does. Many of these messages are so embedded in our socialization patterns that we hardly recognize them. We may also not recognize that we have internalized some stereotype biases or that we express them in our behaviors.

- The statistically significant fact is that we don't have more in common with someone of the same hair color, skin color, or eye color than with someone with different hair, skin, or eye colors.

Homework: Read "The Stereotype Within" by Marc Elrich (2002). Discuss with your learning partner using the questions in the Exercise 17 homework handout.

Exercise 17 Handout: Stereotype Labels

good at math	terrorist	physically well-endowed	alcoholic	can't dance
nerd	class clown	loud	rich	ghetto
lazy	slow	thug	not too smart	financially savvy
athletic	has no rhythm	speaks English poorly	knows martial arts	immigrant
speaks Spanish	violent	poor	listens to rap music	loves watermelon and chicken
illiterate	jealous	deadbeat	jolly	sneaky
angry	on public assistance	dad is a gardener	mom is a maid	hot tempered
has a large family	loves to cook	wears tight and revealing clothes	savage	criminal

Exercise 18: Name Game

Time: 30 minutes

Materials: Exercise 18 homework handout (see p. 194)

Learning Objective: To examine how our names connect with our culture

Facilitator Guidelines:

1. Divide the room into groups of three to four, and provide each person with a name tag.

2. Ask participants to write their full birth name on the name tag and then discuss how they got their name. Some questions to consider include the following:

    - ► Who gave you your name, and why?
    - ► What is the story, if any, behind your name?
    - ► What is the meaning of your name? In what ways does it suit you?
    - ► Who else in your family has this name?
    - ► Discuss how you feel about your name, and why.
    - ► If you could choose another name, which one would you choose, and why?

Whole-Group Debrief:

- What is the association between names and ethnicity?
- In what ways did our names influence our identity development?
- What is the power of names? Do some names have more power than others? If so, which ones, and why?
- Why is it important to call children by the names their parents gave them?
- What other ubiquitous things in our society communicate power—hidden in plain sight?

Homework: Read "Teachers, Please Learn Our Names! Racial Micro-aggressions and the K–12 Classroom" by Rita Kohli and Daniel G. Solórzano (2012). Discuss with your learning partner using the questions in the Exercise 18 homework handout.

Exercise 19: Walk Down Memory Lane

Time: 20 minutes

Materials: Butcher paper, Exercise 19 homework handout (see p. 195)

Learning Objective: To understand the childhood experiences of people as they learned about the social meaning a culture attaches to race

Facilitator Guidelines: Post two extended stretches of butcher paper in the staff lounge or other regular meeting space. In bright marker with large letters, write on one sheet: When was the first time you noticed race or racism and what happened? On the second sheet write: When was the first time you noticed race or racism at a school? Ask staff to write their responses at any time during the week and they may remain anonymous if they choose. Before the next equity meeting, ask staff to walk along the butcher paper walls and read the various posts.

Small-Group Debrief:
- What did you notice?
- How early were some of the experiences?
- Why do you think these experiences "stuck" with people?
- Do you think children of color notice race or racism earlier than white children? Why or why not?
- What were your thoughts as you read the incidences that occurred at a school? How do you believe those incidences affected students or staff of color?
- In your role with students, what could you do to mitigate these kinds of experiences?

Key Takeaways:
- Children are taught by parents, friends, role models, and teachers and through messages in the culture about who is valued and who is not.
- Children of color, on average, recognize how skin color is leveraged to extend social power at an earlier age than children with light skin.
- The alienation and disapproval from peers, teachers, role models, media, and other influences within the culture can be emotionally and psychologically devastating.
- When children do not have to confront social barriers of race, it provides a kind of privilege. People with light skin are granted privileges that people with darker skin are not granted. One of these privileges is the ability to navigate childhood without being maligned, alienated, or denied opportunities because of the color of your skin, your designated race, or the shadow of ethnic stereotypes.

Homework: Read "Unpacking Internalized Racism: Teachers of Color Striving for Racially Just Classrooms" by Rita Kohli (2014). Discuss with your learning partner using the questions in the Exercise 19 homework handout.

Exercise 20: Playing with Dolls

Time: 30 minutes

Materials: The Clark Doll Experiment on YouTube (www.youtube.com/watch?v=tkpUyB2xgTM), Exercise 20 homework handout (see p. 196)

Learning Objective: To discuss internalized racism

Facilitator Guidelines: Have participants watch the Clark Doll Experiment on YouTube. There are numerous ones, including the one above.

Small-Group Discussion:

- Discuss internalized racism and how it relates to the content in this video.
- What evidence of internalized racism did you observe from some of the research participants? How might you recognize it?
- What evidence of implicit bias did you observe from some of the research participants?
- Where might the research participants have received their messages about the value placed on skin color?
- What might be some of the long-term implications for children who experience regular microaggressions that devalue them as a person?
- What can you do to mitigate these experiences for students?

Homework: Read "'They Don't Know Anything!' Latinx Immigrant Children Appropriating the Oppressor's Voice" by Lilia D. Monzó (2016). Discuss with your learning partner using the questions in the Exercise 20 homework handout.

Exercise 21: Lazarus Middle School

Time: 60 minutes

Materials: Exercise 21 handout

Learning Objective: To apply the learning concepts from this quarter in the context of a work environment

Facilitator Guidelines:

1. Pass out the Exercise 21 handout, "Lazarus Middle School" scenario. Ask participants to assign roles and act out the various parts.
2. On completion, have participants discuss the scenario, considering the questions included in the handout.

Small-Group Debrief:

- How should Casey respond?
- What part, if any, are race and culture playing in interactions at Lazarus Middle School?

- What bias, if any, did you hear from staff?
- What role might bias be playing in student achievement?
- What observation might indicate that generational trauma could be in play with students or parents?

In Pairs Only:

- Talk with a partner about Elaine's initial comments about language acquisition. What feelings surfaced when you read her comments, and why?
- What privileges are some students granted at Lazarus that others clearly are not? Why?

Whole-Group Debrief:

- Why is the student population changing at Lazarus, and how is the school adapting to the changes?
- What are the implications if change does not occur?
- What are the cultural challenges that our school faces, and how are we adapting?
- What are the implications if we fail to do so?

To Note in Your Personal Journal:

- Did you recognize any biases you might have expressed in characters in this scenario? If so, what were those biases and where did you learn them? If not, did you recognize them in someone you know? Where might they have learned them?
- How might your biases be influencing your perceptions, behaviors, and decision making?

Key Takeaways:

- Our perceptions, assumptions, biases, beliefs, and values influence our behaviors personally and professionally.
- If our students are not academically successful, we need to interrogate the root of our behaviors—our beliefs.

Homework: Meet with your learning partner to decide if you will stay together another quarter or if you would both prefer to spend some growth time with another learner.

Exercise 21 Handout: "Lazarus Middle School" Scenario

Characters
Elaine, 6th grade English teacher
Andrea, technology teacher
Ken, 7th grade science teacher
Ed, dean of students
Casey, principal

Lazarus Middle School was part of the Bloomingdale School District. In this socioeconomically diverse suburb of a major metropolitan city, 60 percent of the students were on free and reduced-price lunch; the remaining 40 percent were from either middle- or upper-middle-class families. Of the approximately 300 students, 42 percent were white, 18 percent were Black, 30 percent were Hispanic, and 10 percent were Asian.

This was Casey's second year at Lazarus as principal, and this year promised to be quite different from the previous year. The school now qualified to receive Title I funding, and although Casey was excited at the prospect of receiving additional monies to support academic efforts, she wanted to move the school from targeted assistance to schoolwide assistance as quickly as possible to gain more flexibility with how the funds are used. This would require an extensive process of assessing the emerging needs of the school.

One of Casey's first tasks as principal was to meet with her leadership team. As the team assembled for the first time that school year, Casey thanked the team members for their hard work on achievement the previous year and then presented them with the most recent results from the state high-stakes test. It seemed achievement had been declining over the past three years. Reading scores had dived 10 percent, writing scores were down by 13 percent, math scores had decreased by 16 percent, and science proficiency hovered at a dismal 41 percent. As Casey searched the faces of her team for their responses, she cleared her throat: "As we prepare to modify our school improvement plan for this year, we need to consider the current status of achievement and draft a plan to address our needs. So, for starters, to what do you attribute decreasing student achievement at Lazarus?" The following discussion ensued.

Elaine: The student demographics at Lazarus have shifted. When I first started teaching here, this was a neighborhood school. Generations of families attended this school. Now at least half of our students come from everywhere *but* here, and they aren't literate in any language. Most of us teachers don't speak Spanish, Vietnamese, Swahili, or whatever else the students are speaking. What are we supposed to do? If I moved to their country, I'd have to learn their language. Why can't they learn mine? Truth is, we've got a group of kids at this school who probably are struggling to speak, much less learn. It's not surprising the scores are dipping.

Andrea: The issue is not language; it's social class. There's a real division among students. The middle-class students look down on the kids who don't have nice clothes and shoes. Their self-image is so important to them at this age. I'm afraid some of our kids are checking out emotionally *and* academically. They don't want to be here. They don't feel like they belong.

Ed: Maybe they don't. Maybe it's time we start checking immigration status.

Elaine: Well, I am proud that the scores of the honors students have remained high, despite the decline in other subgroups. Casey, as you know, teachers refer students to the honors classes based on their performance in the regular classes. We have had an increasing number of students enrolled in these classes, which provide numerous opportunities for critical thinking and problem solving. It's too bad we have very few students of color enrolled, but I guess that's not surprising if many of them can't speak English well or have not had previous access to these kinds of activities. We all use the same curriculum, though, so they could succeed if they wanted to.

Andrea: Not really. I noticed when I sub in some of my colleagues' classrooms that they use lots of rote and drill worksheets, particularly in the remedial classes that students must take when they are failing other core classes. They might have the same curriculum, but the delivery is very different in some classes.

Ken: Look, I've been teaching here for 18 years. This school is divided, even at recess. Most of the Hispanic kids play soccer during recess. They love it. But we have yet to offer soccer as a regular part of our intermural program. Sure, we've got football, basketball, and wrestling, which lots of kids participate in, but are we failing to recognize the interests of *all* of our students? I don't think we're being as responsive as we could be.

Ed: Well, we're being responsive all right. Every time I turn around, I've got a discipline referral to referee a dispute—one of those kids is always disrespecting one of us. You know they moved here from these gang-infested places where everyone solves disputes with fights and curses. Their parents are no better. Good Lord, it's a mess. I don't care about being politically correct. This is about—

Ken: Whoa, Ed! I'm going to stop you. These days when you point out the obvious, you could lose your job. And we've been working together for 10 years. Let's just say that we see all our students the same way. We treat all our students the same way. We don't know why some students act differently. They just do. We don't know why the scores are down. They just are. We are all out here doing the best we can with what we have. Leave it at that.

Elaine: Maybe it would help if we had some diversity on this staff. Have we even sought to hire teachers of other cultures or races?

Ed: That would be racist. We hire the best person for the job. Period. It is not our policy to consider race in our hiring practices.

Andrea: Well, maybe we could at least hire another ELL teacher to help teach these kids. Some of these kids get teased mercilessly for not speaking good English. Some of them have stopped speaking out in class altogether.

Ken: It's more than that. We have to praise students when they do try and speak. I'm not sure we do much affirming in our instructional practice.

Andrea: That's not our job. We're here to teach. They'll get praised when they do something successful. If we praise them for every little thing, they won't aspire to greater things. We'd only be setting them up with low expectations.

Elaine: Look, the teachers are teaching their heart out. Trouble is, I don't think some of these kids *want* to learn. Yesterday, Patty did this fabulous math lesson on golf. Came straight from our new textbook. But you know what? Some of the students hadn't been to a golf course and tuned out almost immediately.

Andrea: Patty learned her lesson though. The next period, she started by giving a similar example of the concepts, using a pool game. A lot more students got hooked in. She also made sure she taught the key vocabulary and had photos, and she grabbed a pair of clubs from the trunk of her car before she introduced the golf piece. It went much better.

Ken: But that's an excellent point. These parents aren't exposing their kids to a lot of stuff like our parents used to do. Kids are sitting home watching Netflix and playing video games. They don't have the same work ethic and values that we do.

Elaine: I tell you what will get our parents' attention. Make all students pass a rigorous test before they can go on to the next grade. After enough of these kids start failing, the students will start paying attention, and probably more parents will start coming to parent conferences. We just need to get their attention.

Ed: Well, some of these parents aren't very well educated themselves. How am I supposed to communicate with them when they can't even grasp the fundamentals of schooling?

Andrea: I'm thinking we need to take a closer look at that reading program we adopted three years ago. Maybe it's time we switch to something else. You know, Chesapeake County just adopted a new program, and I'm hearing great things about it.

Elaine: Wait! Our teachers have finally gotten to a point where they can use the reading system fluently. Besides, adopting a new reading program doesn't explain why achievement scores have dropped in other content areas. We've already got five new initiatives to implement this year! You think maybe some other things are happening in classrooms to explain these scores? Ed, what are the numbers looking like in discipline?

Ed: Sheesh, we get a lot of referrals for disrespect and insubordination—mostly Black and Hispanic kids. Once I yank them out of class, though, things seem to run more smoothly. Then the kids who want to learn can actually learn.

Elaine: Right, Ed. All these new kids are dragging our scores down. I can't work miracles in one year when they come here three and four years behind everyone else.

Andrea: Bottom line is our scores will improve if we can get more support from administration. The last administration expected teachers to do everything while they sat in their office shuffling papers. We need to continue to come down hard on discipline and raise the rigor of instruction. We've got a solid curriculum, staff members who are committed, and a caring leadership team. Now we just need administration to support the policies and procedures we already have in place.

Ed and Elaine nodded their approval. As the principal drew a deep breath, she considered her response.

As Quarter 1 Draws to a Close . . .

I trust you have learned some salient truths about yourself, your beliefs, your values, and how they inform your behaviors and those of others. We have explored how bias influences our interactions with children and how children can internalize negative messages we convey with bias. And we have learned that racism is more than name calling or prejudicial attitude.

By definition, racism differs from prejudice because it entails a power imbalance in which one party has the power to make decisions or take actions that can have a detrimental, long-term, or even fatal impact on the lives of the targets. It's also bigger than one person. It manifests in institutions and systems that can wield considerable power to subjugate entire communities, usually communities of color.

Take a moment to assess where you are on the "Awaken and Assess" section of the Cultural Competency Continuum (see Figure 4.1). I'm hoping you'll see some areas to celebrate growth and other areas that you may wish to explore further in your professional development opportunities.

Figure 4.1 **Awaken and Assess**

<table>
<tr>
<td rowspan="2">STEP 1. AWAKEN AND ASSESS</td>
<td>Culturally competent professionals acknowledge and continually examine the influence of culture, race, power, and privilege and how that influence manifests itself in their personal and professional decisions.</td>
</tr>
<tr>
<td>

_____I can recognize how past historical actions are affecting current social and economic circumstances.

_____I am aware of my own values, beliefs, stereotypes, and biases.

_____I can recognize how my cultural beliefs and biases may be affecting my decision making, behavior, and perceptions of others.

_____I have unpacked my feelings about language acquisition, language barriers, and language bias and support linguistic diversity.

_____I can recognize privilege in society and organizations.

_____I understand how white privilege and racism affect me and others.

_____I can identify and discuss several strengths of diverse culture, ethnicity, language, and identity.

_____I understand the varied cultural values of my colleagues and students.

_____I recognize the various kinds of racism.

_____I understand the changing racial and ethnic demographics and am prepared to be culturally responsive to all of my students and colleagues.

_____I understand the role of power in organizations and in the construction of race.

_____I affirm and respect cultures other than my own.

_____I value culture as an integral part of a person's identity and maintain cultural curiosity rather than fear or avoidance.

_____I regularly and experientially explore the histories, accomplishments, interests, perceptions, and lived experiences of people with different cultural and racial identities.

_____I actively seek to foster meaningful relationships with people of different cultural and racial identities.
</td>
</tr>
</table>

5

Apply and Act

In this second quarter of the school year, we will begin to transition from an emphasis on understanding ourselves to an emphasis on understanding our influence on students and their holistic well-being. Whether you are working with a culturally diverse or homogenous group of students, their evolving self-identity is shaped in part by how you and others respond to them (Martin, 2014). How they see themselves shapes their choice of attire, their attitude, their motivation, their academic choices, their performance, and their behavior.

Our work as educators is to support their positive identity development by providing experiences that bring them success. One of the best gifts an educator can give students is to help them unwrap their own gifts, talents, and potential. The measure of a great educator is not what or how much they know, but what or how much they give to their students. It's a matter of understanding one's own identity enough to accept, embrace, and nurture another's differences.

Culturally Responsive Pedagogical Practices

Teaching that integrates the culture and interests of students is not a new concept, and it need not be approached like a new initiative or undertaking. A culturally competent educator uses culturally responsive instructional practices. It is not difficult to embed such evidence-based practices in the existing pedagogical framework of your school or district.

A number of researchers laid the groundwork for culturally responsive pedagogy, and numerous others have expanded our understanding of how to meet the needs of students who are culturally and ethnically diverse (Andrews, 2007; Banks et al., 2001; Griner & Stewart, 2013; Ladson-Billings, 1995; Milner, 2010; Sampson & Garrison-Wade, 2011). Culturally responsive teaching, as defined by Gay (2010), has the following characteristics:

- It acknowledges the legitimacy of the cultural heritages of different ethnic groups.
- It builds bridges of meaningfulness between home and school experiences.
- It uses a wide variety of instructional strategies.
- It teaches students to understand and celebrate their cultural heritages.
- It incorporates multicultural information, resources, and materials.

Numerous evidence-based instructional strategies have been identified to support culturally responsive teaching. Here I highlight some promising practices.

The Culturally Responsive Teaching Tool

This checklist of evidence-based teaching strategies and practices is designed by Griner and Stewart (2013) and is comprehensive of teaching, community, parent, and professional practices that have demonstrated success with diverse school populations. A complete copy can be accessed using the article listed in the References.

Culturally Responsive Teaching Strategies

Kieran and Anderson (2018) aligned the strategies identified for culturally responsive teaching with the Universal Design for Learning Framework. The researchers made explicit connections between numerous strategies identified through the literature that support culturally responsive teaching (CRT) and the UDL framework. Using the culturally responsive teaching strategies they identified, one could contextualize it by analyzing where each of these strategies may fit in other instructional frameworks you are using such as Marzano's (2007) or Danielson's (2007). The strategies identified for culturally responsive teaching are good teaching practices for all students.

Culturally responsive teaching is simply good teaching; any notion that it will take years to implement is simply not true. We can all integrate culturally responsive teaching into our current teaching practices. All it takes is effort and intention. In Exercise 23, you will conduct a similar analysis with the pedagogical framework used most often in your school or district.

Now it's cultural competency in schools and classrooms—full speed ahead!

Exercises for Quarter 2

Following are 13 exercises that will help you *apply and act* on what you will be learning about culturally responsive pedagogical practices during this second quarter.

Exercise 22: Using Culturally Responsive Teaching Tenets

Time: 60 minutes

Materials: Exercise 22 handout. **Note:** Teachers may need administrative support in covering classes so learning partners can video each other during this weeklong exercise.

Learning Objective: To learn from one another how to use culturally responsive teaching tenets in the classroom

Facilitator Guidelines:

1. Divide participants into groups of four to five.

2. In small groups, discuss ways the strategies have or would be employed in a classroom.

3. Now have each group member team up with their learning partner and arrange a time that they can video their partner modeling a 20-minute lesson using some of the culturally responsive strategies with students.

4. For the next few cultural competency sessions, each group presents their videos. Each teacher should introduce the strategy they are modeling and share tips for implementing it effectively. Continue each week until every group has presented and staff have seen each strategy demonstrated by a colleague.

Whole-Group Debrief: Each group presents a specific example of how they used the strategies in their personal practice.

Homework: Video your learning partner using one or more culturally responsive teaching strategies.

Exercise 22 Handout: Culturally Responsive Teaching Strategies

Culturally Diverse Materials/Resources/Curriculum
Visual, auditory, and multimedia representations to reduce barriers to print
Digital and visual literacies taught
Resources with multiple perspectives throughout the year, including race/race history as part of the curriculum (Fiedler et al., 2008; Howard & Novarro, 2016)
Draw on primary resources from multiple perspectives
Learning Environment That Promotes Positive Identity Development
Diversity (in the classroom and the community) is taught as a strength
Attitudes and instructional approaches demonstrate that intelligence is expandable
Students share knowledge, traditions, and experiential knowledge through storytelling, family histories and biographies, chronicles, and other narratives (Howard & Navarro, 2016; Yosso, 2005)
Cultural capital from within the community is used (Yosso, 2005)
Students learn active citizenship for authentic problem-solving and social justice (DeCuir-Gunby, Taliaferro, & Greenfield, 2010)
Students create affirmations and express their values associated with learning (Steele, 2010)
Educators communicate high expectations in students' ability to master rigorous standards (Steele, 2010; Tatum, 1997)
An environment of mutual respect among peers and between students and staff (Ginsberg, 2005)
Mistakes are communicated as opportunities that are a part of learning; effort, not ability, is promoted (Marzano, Pickering, & Pollock, 2001; Tatum, 1997)
Positive and proactive behavior supports are in place, behavioral expectations are clear (Fiedler et al., 2008)
Direct Instruction
Explicit instruction of new vocabulary with concrete or visual representations and multiple opportunities to use the words (Piazza, Rao, & Protacio, 2015)
Assignments allow students to construct knowledge and make meaning of their world
Metacognitive strategies are taught that help students when they encounter learning challenges
Examples and analogies from students' lives are integrated into the lesson (Villegas & Lucas, 2002)
Minimal distractions with sustained thought of critical material
A Community of Learners
Cross-cultural conversations that challenge the dominant perspective (Howard & Navarro, 2016)
Collective, cooperative, and collaborative learning with supportive relationships
Reciprocal strategies are used to discuss new content, learn from peers, and increase students' oral language usage, fluency, and comprehension (Piazza et al., 2015)
Independent Practice
Allow for student choice on assignments/topics to increase personal relevance (Ginsberg, 2005)
Assessment
Corrective feedback from the teacher is clearly and explicitly framed by and connected to high standards

Source: Adapted from "Connecting Universal Design for Learning with Culturally Responsive Teaching," L. Kieran and C. Anderson, 2018, *Education and Urban Society*, pp. 10–11. Copyright 2018 by L. Kieran and C. Anderson. Used with permission of SAGE Publications, Inc.

Exercise 23: Culturally Responsive Teaching and Teaching Frameworks

Time: 40 minutes

Materials: Your school district teaching framework, Exercise 22 handout ("Culturally Responsive Teaching Strategies")

Learning Objective: To analyze how culturally responsive teaching tenets align with your current teaching framework

Facilitator Guidelines:

1. Have participants divide into groups of four to five. Ask each group to take the 24 tenets of culturally responsive teaching from the Exercise 22 handout of culturally responsive teaching strategies and see where each of those strategies might fit in the school's or district's current teaching framework.

2. Each group should compile its own list.

3. Have participants make a copy of their list and post it online or in the teachers' lounge so others can compare notes.

Homework: Read "It's Not Hard Work; It's Heart Work: Strategies of Effective, Award-Winning Culturally Responsive Teachers" by Abiola Farinde-Wu, Crystal P. Glover, and Nakeshia N. Williams (2017).

With your learning partner, discuss the five foundational factors that award-winning teachers employ. Which of these strategies, if any, would work in your classroom? Why or why not? How would you modify these strategies to meet the needs of your students?

Exercise 24: Double Jeopardy

Time: 35 minutes

Materials: Exercise 24 handout

Learning Objective: To explore how the history of various Americans is portrayed in American curricula, text, and educational contexts

Facilitator Guidelines:

1. In groups of three to four, have participants complete the Exercise 24 handout, which matches prominent American citizens from various eras of U.S. history to their specific accomplishments. Participants will have 10 minutes. See how many you can match without using your smartphone or Wikipedia. Don't worry. You will be able to use them later as part of your homework exercise.

2. After 10 minutes, pass out the answer sheet and facilitate discussion by asking the following questions:

> ► How many of you were able to make the correct matches for the first category without technological assistance (100 points)?

> ► How many of you were able to make the correct matches for the other categories without technological assistance?

> ► Why do you know more about the contributions of American people with lighter skin than about the contributions of American people with darker skin? How did that happen? Why did that happen?

> ► Why is it important that students know the contributions that *all* Americans have made to this country? Why would both the historical and recent accomplishments of people from every racial and ethnic background be important to all students?

Key Takeaways:

• People from all racial categories made significant contributions to our country. However, it was primarily the accomplishments of people with light skin that were documented in history books and included in school curricula.

• Colonizers systematically stripped oppressed peoples of their culture by deliberately excluding their history from history books. It was also common to ban the use of native languages, dress, customs, and religious practices. Subsequently, this practice disrupted the positive self-identity development of marginalized people, leading many Americans to believe that most of the major contributions in this country came from people with lighter skin—bolstering the lies of superiority.

• The fact that many struggle with identifying the contributions of American people with darker skin is evidence of the long-term effects of these practices.

Exercise 24 Handout: Double Jeopardy

Match the correct names in the list below with the accomplishments listed in the table. Use the number beside each name to identify the person in question. Smartphone and Wikipedia use is encouraged. Post your answers online or in a shared space for staff learning.

Names of Americans Who Made Important Contributions to the World

1. Neil Armstrong
2. George Edward Alcorn Jr.
3. Luis Walter Alvarez
4. Fred Begay
5. Regina Benjamin
6. Hillary Clinton
7. Charles Curtis
8. Christine Chen
9. Elaine Chao
10. David L. Chew
11. Min Chueh Chang
12. Amelia Earhart
13. Alberto Gonzales
14. Charles Alexander Eastman
15. David G. Farragut
16. Ira Hayes
17. John Bennett Herrington
18. Daniel Inouye

19. John F. Kennedy
20. Antonia Novello
21. Shirley Ann Jackson
22. Robert Cornelius Murphy
23. Abraham Lincoln
24. Walter McAfee
25. Ellen Ochoa
26. Sacagawea
27. Sonia Sotomayor
28. Mark Twain
29. Harriet Tubman
30. Maria Tallchief
31. Robert Parris Moses
32. George Washington
33. Kristi Yamaguchi
34. Elwood Quesada
35. Guion Stewart Bluford Jr.

	White Americans	Black or African Americans	American Indians/Native Americans	Asian Americans/Native Hawaiian/Pacific Islander	Hispanic/Latin American
100 Points	First person to walk on the moon. Who is it? # _____	Theoretical physicist and famous inventor; has been credited with making many advances in science, including portable fax and touch-tone phones Who is it? # _____	Traveled with the famous Lewis and Clark expedition Who is it? # _____	Internet entrepreneur and engineer; co-created Snapchat. In 2015, became the second-youngest billionaire in the world Who is it? # _____	1968 Nobel Prize in Physics for discoveries about subatomic particles; later, proposed the now-accepted theory that the mass dinosaur extinction was caused by a meteor impact Who is it? # _____
200 Points	Former U.S. Secretary of State Who is it? # _____	Aerospace engineer, retired U.S. Air Force officer and fighter pilot, and former NASA astronaut Who is it? # _____	Was a member of the Iwo Jima Flag Raising during World War II Who is it? # _____	Won three national figure skating championships, two world titles, and the 1992 Olympic gold medal Who is it? # _____	Physician, 14th U.S. Surgeon General Who is it? # _____
300 Points	Played a role in diffusing the Cuban missile crisis and the threat of nuclear war Who is it? # _____	Physicist and inventor who invented a method of fabricating an S-ray spectrometer and other notable inventions Who is it? # _____	Retired United States Naval Aviator and former NASA astronaut Who is it? # _____	Captain, U.S. Army; Senator; Medal of Honor recipient World War II Who is it? # _____	U.S. Supreme Court Justice Who is it? # _____
400 Points	Flew solo across the Atlantic Ocean in 1932 Who is it? # _____	Used his MacArthur Fellowship to start the Algebra Project, a national mathematics literacy program for high school Who is it? # _____	Nuclear physicist whose work was in the alternative use of laser, electron, and ion beams to heat thermonuclear plasmas for use as alternative energy sources Who is it? # _____	Emmy Award-winning journalist and news anchor Who is it? # _____	Former U.S. Attorney General Who is it? # _____
500 Points	Was an American author and humorist Who is it? # _____	During the Civil War, served as an armed scout and spy for the U.S. Army Who is it? # _____	Danced for the Ballet Russe de Monte Carlo and the New York City Ballet Who is it? # _____	Former Secretary of Labor Who is it? # _____	Helped create the Federal Aviation Administration Who is it? # _____
600 Points	Led the Union forces during the American Civil War Who is it? # _____	Scientist and astronomer, notable for participating in the world's first lunar radar echo experiments with Project Diana Who is it? # _____	Former Vice President of the United States Who is it? # _____	White House Staff Secretary under President Ronald Reagan Who is it? # _____	Logged nearly 1,000 hours in space; co-inventor on three patents for optical inspection systems Who is it? # _____
700 Points	Served as Commander in Chief of American forces during the Revolutionary War Who is it? # _____	18th U.S. Surgeon General Who is it? # _____	Physician, writer, national lecturer, and co-founder of the Boy Scouts of America Who is it? # _____	Co-inventor of the combined oral contraceptive pill Who is it? # _____	First U.S. naval officer ever to be awarded the rank of admiral Who is it? # _____
Total Points					

Exercise 25: A Look at Cultural Identities

Time: 15 minutes

Materials: Exercise 25 homework handout (see p. 197)

Learning Objective: To explore how teaching is influenced by cultural norms

Facilitator Guidelines:

1. Tell participants that they will be solving a problem that occurred at a real school. Have them divide into groups of four to five for discussion.

2. Read aloud the following scenario. Have participants discuss their thoughts in their groups and decide as a group on the best approach for dealing with the issue.

3. After five minutes, ask each group to discuss their approach to solving the issue. When all solutions have been presented, participants should constructively critique the responses of their peers.

Scenario: Mr. Albert's Communication Style

Mr. Albert is a popular teacher who is well-liked by students. In team meetings, however, he draws the ire of some colleagues. His voice is loud and might be considered dominating. Anxious to make an important point, he is known to frequently interrupt a speaker. Excited about a topic, he sometimes talks or laughs over others. Some staff find these behaviors very annoying and have complained to his supervisor.

As a member of his team, what would be the culturally responsive way to resolve this issue? You have five minutes to discuss a strategic approach.

Whole-Group Debrief:

- Was this behavior a cultural norm? How might you determine that?
- How do you collaborate with people who may have different cultural norms or expectations than you? What do you do if they disagree with you?
- Is it your role to teach cultural norms? If so, when and how?

Key Takeaways:

- It is not unusual to assume that behavior that differs from your own is unacceptable or inappropriate. But "appropriate" behavior is subject to cultural norms. What may be acceptable in one culture may not be acceptable in another, and vice versa.
- There are several cultures and subcultures where Mr. Albert's communication style is accepted and promoted as appropriate, if not preferential. It would not be culturally responsive to assume that one norm is superior to another.

- To determine if this is a cultural norm, speak with Mr. Albert privately and ask him about the cultural norms he formed in interactions with family and community members. When you have a better understanding of how or why he uses the communication patterns he does, you can transition the conversation into sharing your own communication patterns and how they differ from his.

- Ask him if the two of you can work together to find a middle ground in which both of your communication styles are respected. Share the power equally.

- This conversation should occur before any reports are shared with his supervisor. To report him to his supervisor without attempting to resolve this issue with him directly is disrespectful, unfair, and not inclusive.

- You should teach cultural norms only when someone requests it. Mr. Albert is likely already aware of your norms, but there are two norms at play in this scenario, and each one deserves acceptance.

Homework: Read "'The Fish Becomes Aware of the Water in Which It Swims': Revealing the Power of Culture in Shaping Teaching Identity" by Yuli Rahmawati and Peter C. Taylor (2018). Complete the Exercise 25 homework handout before meeting with your learning partner to discuss.

Exercise 26: Songs of Praise

Time: 45 minutes

Materials: Personal journals, Exercise 26 handout

Learning Objective: To model a strategy for reinforcing positive self-identity with students

Facilitator Guidelines:

1. Send an e-mail to participants a week in advance, asking them to meet with their homework learning partners to identify key information or descriptive words relative to their partner's culture, ethnicity, language, and identity (see Exercise 26 handout).

2. Using the information from their brief interview, each participant must compose a short song about their learning partner. Popular tunes are suggested as a guide.

3. Each participant performs their short composition in small groups of four to five people during this session. The best songs from each group will be performed before the whole group.

Whole-Group Debrief:

- How did you feel when you heard your song?

- What is the value of recognizing and celebrating the unique characteristics, talents, and strengths of another person?

- How do you or how could you recognize and celebrate the unique characteristics, talents, and strengths of all your students?
- How would you modify or adapt this activity for your students?

Key Takeaways:

- Every person in the school should feel accepted, even when they experience failure, disappointments, or challenges.
- Every person in the school should feel appreciated and celebrated for their unique talents and gifts.
- Staff and faculty need a process or strategy for identifying someone's unique talents and gifts.
- Activities such as this help people separate a person's identity, which encompasses their potential, from a person's behavior, which may not always reflect who they are or what they have the potential to become.

Exercise 26 Handout: Songs of Praise

The story is told of a tribe in Africa in which a rich tradition thrives. When a child is named, the parents and extended family compose a song about the child. The song may explain the meaning behind the name, the potential the child has, the talents and gifts that are endowed, or the history or achievements of the family. In short, the song praises the identity and potential of the child. The song is revealed at a special ceremony for the entire community.

The song will be repeated many times during the life of the person. For example, when the mother rocks the child to sleep, she may sing the song. Or when the father comes home from work, he may sing the song. But one of the most important occasions for singing the song is when the child makes a mistake or commits an act that hurts themselves, others, or the community. It's when the person may feel the most isolated or ashamed that the community gathers together and sings the child or adult their song. The song is meant to remind the person that they are so much more than their failures or shortcomings.

Your role today is to compose a song for your learning partner. Using the prompts below, interview your learning partner to help guide the content you may choose to include in your song. You will reveal your song to your partner in small groups with your colleagues at your next meeting. Good luck, and have fun!

Learning Partner's Name: _____

Suggested Tunes to Use for the Song: "Row, Row, Row Your Boat," "Twinkle, Twinkle, Little Star," "London Bridge Is Falling Down," "Mary Had a Little Lamb," "Three Blind Mice"

Three Values from Your Partner's Culture:

Your Partner's Ethnicity:

Languages Your Partner Can Speak:

Three Positive Words Your Partner Uses to Describe Themselves:

Three Positive Words You Might Use to Describe Your Partner:

Exercise 27: Race to Review

Time: 60 minutes

Materials: Student office referrals from first quarter, Exercise 27 homework handout (see p. 198)

Learning Objective: To analyze data for patterns in student behavior office referrals

Facilitator Guidelines:

1. Ask participants to organize by grade level or content area.
2. Provide copies of specific student office referrals for shared students in each group. You will need one office referral for each participant in a group. For example, if you have five people in a group, you will need five different student office referrals.
3. Ask each participant to take one referral.
4. Provide three minutes for each participant to read a referral and note similarities between it and the previous referral (after the second round) before passing it to the right.
5. After each participant has read and reviewed each of the referrals in this round, spread all the referrals on the table and discuss your observations.
6. After discussion, you may play as many rounds as you deem appropriate. Each round would require another set of student office referrals.

Guiding Questions for Discussion:

- What did you see?
- Who is being referred to the office for disciplinary action?
- What kinds of disciplinary infractions are noted for office referral?
- How have we cooperatively defined the behavioral infractions?
- When are students being referred to the office for behavioral referral?
- Where are students when the disciplinary infractions occur?
- Are there any similarities in the kinds of students who are referred?
- Are we able to categorize these referrals in any way?
- What patterns, if any, are emerging?
- What strategies can we agree to use to disrupt inequitable patterns?

Whole-Group Debrief:

- What patterns, if any, were observed in your group?
- To what do you attribute these patterns?
- What strategies does your group use to ensure all students receive equitable treatment in class?

- What does equity in disciplinary responses look like? How have we defined it? How will we know when we have achieved it?
- What other data might we review that will help triangulate or deepen our understanding of potential patterns in how we respond to perceived student misbehavior?

Key Takeaways:

- We can analyze and review equity in classroom practices through the lens of documented office referrals.
- Staff members can share successful strategies for working with specific students.
- To achieve consistency across classrooms, we must define what equitable treatment looks and sounds like for all students.
- Disciplinary equity, like all other goals, must be defined, strategized, planned, and monitored for progress and success to occur.

Homework: Read "More Than a Metaphor: The Contribution of Exclusionary Discipline to a School-to-Prison Pipeline" by Russell J. Skiba, Mariella I. Arredondo, and Natasha T. Williams (2014). Discuss with your learning partner using the questions in the Exercise 27 homework handout.

Exercise 28: A Cultural Environment Scavenger Hunt

Time: Two weeks

Materials: Smartphone; PowerPoint, Prezi, or similar presentation software

Learning Objective: To understand the unique cultural environment of the school community

Facilitator Guidelines: The goal of this activity is to acquaint staff members with relevant contextual cultural knowledge about the community they serve. Often staff may not live in the community in which they work. The expectation of this assignment is to integrate this knowledge into instructional practices, curricular resources, learning environments, and outreach with parents.

1. Divide staff into five groups. Each group will have a different set of tasks to complete. Many of these tasks will involve speaking with people in the community. If staff are uncomfortable reaching out to people they don't know, they might use this culturally respectful script: "Hi. I work at XYZ School. I am interested in learning more about the community I serve. Would you be willing to share with me anything you think would be important for me to know?" They have one week to collect evidence of task completion.

2. Have participants use their smartphones to digitally record the completion of each task; they should then load all evidence into a visual presentation. They may complete the tasks together in teams or through individual delegation, but all tasks must be completed.

3. The following week, ask each group to present on the tasks they completed. As a whole group, discuss the cultural knowledge participants learned about the community during the scavenger hunt.

Group One

- Talk with an author/writer/journalist from the school's community. Record them discussing what it was like to grow up there.
- Clip an article from the local newspaper. (The more local, the better.) What does it say about the community?
- Clip a tweet from a legislator who represents that community. What are the most salient issues he or she is trying to tackle?
- Visit the home of a student. (Complete in pairs or as a group.)
- Learn a phrase in the home language of one of your students.
- Talk with a social worker who works in the community.

Group Two

- Attend a service in one of the community's places of worship or talk with one of the community's religious leaders.
- Find a public sculpture or work of art in the community. What is the story behind it?
- Visit the university closest to the community. How many people from the community choose to attend that institution each year?
- Think like a tourist. Find the top three most interesting things to see in the community.
- Take a photo of a display window of a retail store in the community.
- Talk with a mental health professional who works in the community.

Group Three

- Talk to someone at a senior center in the community.
- Visit a restaurant in the community.
- Visit the public library in the community. Find a book about the community.
- Learn a phrase in the home language of one of your students.
- Volunteer in a homeless shelter in or near the community.
- Talk with a medical professional who works in the community.

Group Four

- Visit a museum or cultural center in the community.
- Visit the closest vocational or community college to the community. What are the requirements for entry?
- Visit a business in the community. Why did they choose to locate in this community?
- Ride public transportation in the community.
- Visit another school in the community. How is it similar to and different from the school you work in?
- Talk to a banker who works in the community.

Group Five

- Have coffee with one of your student's parents who grew up in the community.
- Drive around the community. Take pictures of cultural artifacts.
- Visit the home of one of your students. (Complete in pairs or as a group.)
- Visit a barber shop or beauty shop in the community.
- Talk to a police officer who works in the community.
- Talk to a real estate agent who works in the community.

Whole-Group Debrief:

- What surprised you, and what did not?
- What have we learned, and how can we use this learning?
- How can we archive our learning from this week for future access?

Key Takeaways:

- Each community is rich with cultural knowledge. Use this knowledge in your teaching practices.
- Each community has shared values and beliefs. Use this knowledge to better understand your students and their behaviors—especially those behaviors that your students have culturally embraced but that differ from your own. These might include behaviors related to voice tone, greetings, or eye contact, as well as nonverbal behaviors.
- The learning environment should reflect artifacts of pride important to the community and images representative of the ethnic cultures in the community.
- Parent outreach should reflect the needs and interests of parents in the community.

Exercise 29: A Cultural Message Scavenger Hunt

Time: 40 minutes

Materials: None

Learning Objective: To understand the cultural messages in the school

Facilitator Guidelines:

1. Divide the staff into four teams. Send one team in each direction within the school: north, south, east, and west. They have 20 minutes to walk around the entire school and examine the messages on the walls, doors, and bulletin boards and in any other types of signage.

2. As they consider each message, participants should ask themselves if the message favors one culture over another. If so, how?

3. After 20 minutes, reconvene as a whole group to discuss the findings and next steps.

Whole-Group Debrief:

- What surprised you?
- What are we communicating well?
- What can we communicate better?
- How well are the cultural values of the community represented in our environment? (Those discussed by parents and students during our previous interviews.)
- What patterns emerged, if any?
- What are our next steps, and how will we hold ourselves accountable for completing them?

Exercise 30: Talking with Students About Racism

Time: One week

Materials: Exercise 30 handout

Learning Objective: To discuss criminalization of activities by people of color and develop a lesson plan to discuss it

Facilitator Guidelines:

1. Read aloud the recap of Audra D. S. Burch's 2018 *New York Times* article, "How 'Gardening While Black' Almost Landed This Detroit Man in Jail."

2. Ask participants to brainstorm other instances of which they are aware when someone called the police on a person of color for doing an ordinary activity (e.g., sleeping in dorm, waiting at coffee shop, barbecuing in the park, selling bottles of water).

3. Ask participants to develop a lesson plan for students at their preferred grade level that discusses the criminalization of people of color. They may use the basic template provided in the Exercise 30 handout, which includes a feedback rubric at the end, or a template of their choosing (perhaps a standardized district template). Participants may work with their learning partner to develop their lesson, but each person must submit their own lesson.

4. After one week, each participant should come prepared to teach their lesson, bringing any materials they may need. As participants enter the meeting, ask them to deposit a copy of their lesson plan, with their name clearly indicated on it, in a designated container.

5. When all participants are in attendance, randomly select a lesson plan from the container. The educator selected must teach their whole-group lesson to their peers. Following the lesson, peers may provide feedback using the rubric. This can be done in several rounds, depending on your time limitations.

Recap of "How 'Gardening While Black' Almost Landed This Detroit Man in Jail"

Mr. Peeples loved to garden, so he built a beautiful vegetable garden at a neighborhood park. This did not sit well with several nearby neighbors, however. They called the police on him and reported that he had threatened them. They accused him of vandalizing nearby houses and trees and even sexually assaulting them.

Naturally, Mr. Peeples was confused by these allegations because they were completely false. He couldn't rationalize why these neighbors, three women, would make these statements without provocation—except for the fact that Mr. Peeples happened to be Black and the neighbors happened to be white. After multiple calls had been made to the police, Mr. Peeples was charged with stalking the women. Subsequently, he hired an attorney to defend himself against the charges. After several months, a state district judge determined that the accusations were false and were rooted in racism. He dismissed the case. It turns out the three women had plans of their own for the park and used the police to intimidate and harass the gardener.

This story highlights some of the conflict that can occur when neighborhoods are gentrified, forcing or policing out longtime residents. Additionally, police have been used to protect white privileges and criminalize people of color, often for ordinary acts. The women's claims could not be substantiated, but had the judge found them credible, their lies may have cost Mr. Peeples his livelihood, career, and future. In fact, thousands of people of color are in prison today, convicted on claims that could not be substantiated. There has been loss of life in many cases. Mr. Peeples did not lose his life or his freedom, but he suffered other losses—the loss of potential income from future clients who heard about the charges and refused to do business with him and the loss of the fees he paid to his attorney for his defense.

Whole-Group Debrief (to be facilitated *after* the lessons have been developed and taught in whole group):

- What was the role of power in Mr. Peeples's situation? What power did the women accusers wield? What systems and institutions had the power to levy long-term implications for any or all of the parties? Which party bore the brunt of the false accusations? What is the role of power in acts of racism?
- What are some of the challenges of developing lessons that deepen students' understanding of social or racial injustice?
- What common instructional approaches did you use in today's lesson that you have used in other content areas? What, if anything, was different?
- What culturally responsive strategies were integrated in the lessons taught?
- Unfortunately, we could not see everyone's lesson presentation. What are some strategies you used in the development of your lesson presentation that we missed? What were some enduring understandings you sought to teach?

Key Takeaways:

- There are enduring understandings about cultural beliefs and values, racism, and the racialized lives of people that students need to understand. Teaching about them requires many of the same skills you use as a content teacher.
- You can teach short, succinct lessons on current issues. Like anything, it takes practice.

Follow Up: Post all lesson plans online internally for staff to see and provide feedback.

Exercise 30 Handout: Cultural Competency Lesson Plan

My Cultural Competency Lesson Plan for Students	Grade Level:
Outcomes: *What do you want students to know or be able to do as a result of this lesson?* Choose one or more of the items below.	
Enduring Understanding:	
Assessment: *How will you know if students grasped the intended outcome?*	
Learning Plan: *What activities will you do to help them learn the outcome? (10–15 minutes)*	

Cultural Competency Lesson Plan Feedback Rubric	No	Yes
Did the educator explain the goal/outcome and its importance?		
Did the instructor link the content to prior knowledge?		
Were the learning activities clear, relevant, interactive, and inclusive of adequate time to process thinking?		
Did the instructor link the new learning to current or future application using concrete examples?		
Did the students achieve the intended outcome?		
Did the instructor avoid the use of stereotypes, bias, or racialized assumptions?		
Did the instructor establish and reinforce the conditions for a respectful and inclusive learning environment?		
Did the instructor check for understanding?		
Did the instructor use contextual examples, models, graphic organizers, teaching aids, or other visual aids?		
Did students have ample opportunity to talk with one another?		
Did the instructor demonstrate enthusiasm for the topic?		
Good Job! General Feedback:		
Recommendations for Improvement (we all can improve):		

Exercise 31: The Power of a Narrative, Part A

Time: 20 minutes

Materials: Exercise 31 handout

Learning Objective: To surface how participants explain to themselves and one another the reason for academic, disciplinary, or socioeconomic inequities among students with different skin colors

Facilitator Guidelines:

1. Ask participants to organize into small groups, and pass out the national student data by racial categories, as shown in the Exercise 31 handout.

2. Ask participants to review and analyze the data using the questions in the handout. They have 10 minutes to review and discuss.

Whole-Group Debrief:

- Synthesize what you read, observed, and discussed.
- What makes narratives so powerful, and who are they benefitting?
- What can we do when we recognize that narratives are impeding equitable opportunities for students?

Key Takeaways:

- False narratives that assign intellectual, personality, or character traits to people who share common physical characteristics promote practices that perpetuate inequitable outcomes.
- It is important to recognize, challenge, and examine our narratives and their roots.

Exercise 31 Handout: Data and the Power of Narrative

Discussion Questions

- How do you explain these data?
- Is there still inequity in our society? If so, in what does it consist and where is it visible?
- We have talked about how narratives were created to explain the injustices perpetrated against people of color in this country, but what about our own narratives? What have we told ourselves or one another when we try to explain why these kinds of inequities still exist?
- What have we told ourselves about why some groups of students receive different disciplinary treatment than others?
- What reasons have we used to explain why some groups of students make up the vast majority of those who are in poverty or receive free and reduced-price lunch?
- What narratives are we holding on to, and why?

Average National Assessment of Educational Progress (NAEP) Reading Scale Scores of 4th Grade Students, by Race/Ethnicity: Selected Years, 1992–2017

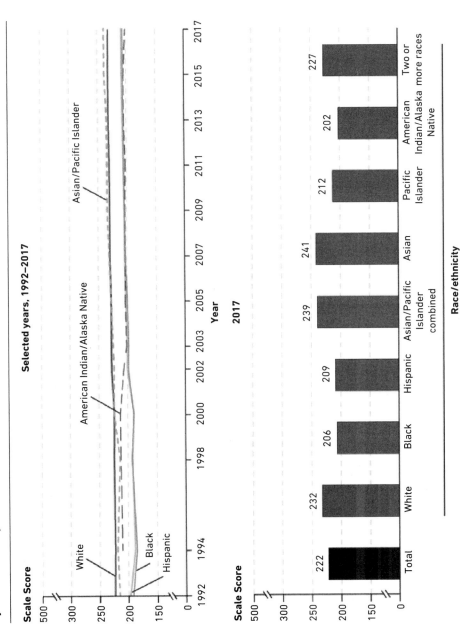

Source: From "From Status and Trends in the Education of Racial and Ethnic Groups. Indicator 10: Reading Achievement," 2019c, National Center for Education Statistics.

Percentage of Children Under Age 18 in Families Living in Poverty Based on the Official Poverty Measure, by Race/Ethnicity: 2000 Through 2016

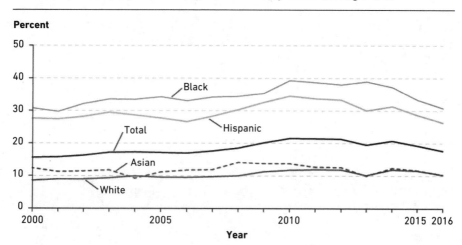

Source: From "Status and Trends in the Education of Racial and Ethnic Groups. Indicator 4: Children Living in Poverty," 2019b, National Center for Education Statistics.

Percentage of Elementary and Secondary School Students Retained in Grade, by Race/Ethnicity: 2000–2016

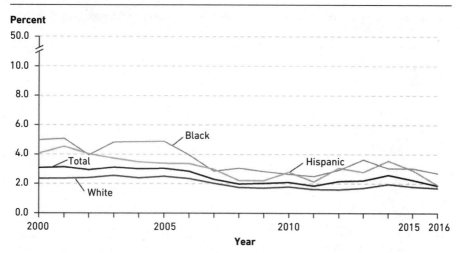

Source: From "Status and Trends in the Education of Racial and Ethnic Groups. Indicator 15: Retention, Suspension, Expulsion," 2019d, National Center for Education Statistics.

Percentage of Public School Students Who Received Out-of-School Suspensions, by Race/Ethnicity and Sex: 2013–14

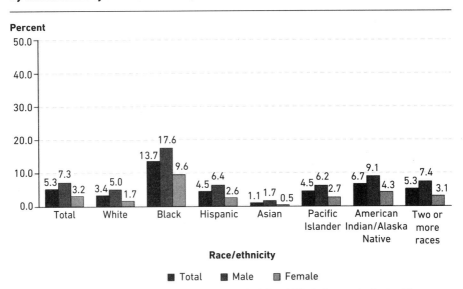

Source: From "Status and Trends in the Education of Racial and Ethnic Groups. Indicator 15: Retention, Suspension, Expulsion," 2019e, National Center for Education Statistics.

Percentage Distribution of Teachers in Public Elementary and Secondary Schools, by Race/Ethnicity: School Years 2003–04 and 2015–16

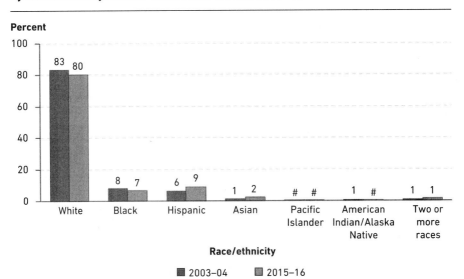

Source: From "Status and Trends in the Education of Racial and Ethnic Groups. Spotlight A: Characteristics of Public School Teachers by Race/Ethnicity," 2019f, National Center for Education Statistics.

Exercise 32: The Power of a Narrative, Part B

Time: 20 minutes

Materials: Student data from your school by racial categories on academic outcomes, discipline (suspensions, expulsions), and poverty (free and reduced-price lunch [see Exercise 31 handout]); paper and markers; three large sheets of butcher paper or large sticky notes taped to the wall, with each one displaying one of these three labels: Academic Narratives, Disciplinary Narratives, and Socioeconomic Narratives

Learning Objective: To surface how participants explain to themselves and one another the reason for academic, disciplinary, or socioeconomic inequities among students with different skin colors

Facilitator Guidelines:

1. Have participants organize into small groups. Pass out the data, paper, and markers.

2. Ask participants to review the data provided in the Exercise 31 handout. Have each participant write down a narrative that might address a given issue. For example, a common narrative is that students with low academic performance are frequently absent from school.

3. Have participants post their narratives on the wall under the label that corresponds to their topic (academic, disciplinary, socioeconomic).

4. Allow time for a gallery walk so others can read the narratives that have been posted.

5. Explain to participants that they can challenge any of the narratives posted. For example, a participant may probe or challenge the narrative concerning poor academic performance and absenteeism from school by writing, "How many days, on average, are these students absent from school?"

6. After 10 minutes, ask participants to synthesize what they read and observed.

Small-Group Debrief:

- How do you explain these data?

- Is there inequity in our learning environment? If so, where?

- We have talked about how narratives were created to explain the injustices perpetrated against people of color in this country, but what about our own narratives? What have we told ourselves or one another when we try to explain why some children have vastly different academic outcomes than others, even when taught by the same teachers?

- What have we told ourselves to explain why some groups of students receive different disciplinary treatment than others, even when they represent a smaller percentage of the total school population?
- What reasons have we used to explain why some groups of students make up the vast majority of those who receive free and reduced-price lunch?

Whole-Group Debrief:

- What makes narratives so powerful, and what can we do when we recognize they are impeding opportunities for students?
- What patterns, problems, or questions did we identify that need further probing?
- Where shall we archive the data for further consideration and inclusion in our equity plans or school improvement plans?

Key Takeaways:

- It is important to monitor and evaluate how well we are providing equitable education for all our students.
- It is equally important to take measured steps to eradicate inequities demonstrated through the interpretation of collected data.

Exercise 33: Memories

Time: 20 minutes

Materials: Exercise 33 homework handout (see p. 199)

Learning Objective: To explore the centrality of injustice and mistreatment

Facilitator Guidelines:

1. Ask participants to recall childhood memories and familial relationships in which they experienced injustice or mistreatment. In pairs, have them share one especially painful experience with a partner. Exercise empathetic listening during this exercise so that listening partners use their time mostly listening, aside from empathetic comments.

2. Each partner has five minutes to share before the pair debrief.

Pair Debrief:

- Was the person who inflicted the mistreatment important to you? Would that have made a difference in how you felt? Why or why not?
- In what way, if any, was the experience dehumanizing?
- Talk about pain as part of the human experience.
- What questions came to mind as your partner told their experience?

- Were you able to identify with your partner's experience in any way?
- What do you think it might feel like to experience pain, mistreatment, or insults by others on a regular, if not daily, basis? What do you imagine might be the long-term effects on a person's emotional state?
- How can you find out if some of your students are experiencing pain or mistreatment from others? What are you willing to do to stop it?

Homework: Read "Becoming a More Culturally Responsive Teacher by Identifying and Reducing Microaggressions in Classrooms and School Communities" by Jacqueline Darvin (2018). Discuss with your learning partner using the questions in the Exercise 33 homework handout.

Exercise 34: Fatigue at Ferdinand High

Time: 35 minutes

Materials: Personal journals, Exercise 34 handout

Learning Objective: To practice how to identify, apply, and act in support of culturally responsive practices

Facilitator Guidelines:

1. Have participants read the "Fatigue at Ferdinand High" scenario in the Exercise 34 handout.
2. Participants will then discuss the scenario in small groups, in a whole group, and in pairs.
3. Participants will reflect on several questions in their journals.
4. At the conclusion of the discussion, have learning partners decide whether they would like to remain together or switch to another learning partner for the next quarter.

Small-Group Debrief:

- Using the White Racial Identity Development Model from Chapter 2 (see p. 29), analyze where each of the characters is in their development.
- What skills, behaviors, and dispositions need to be addressed at Ferdinand High, if any?
- What practices, procedures, and policies need to be reviewed at Ferdinand High, if any?
- The staff has been learning about cultural competency. How are they using that knowledge with students? How does their knowledge influence school policies and practices?
- What do these teachers need to learn next, and how should they learn it?

Whole-Group Debrief:

- How would you have managed Wendy's classroom situation better?
- What issues do we still need to address at our school?
- What policies and practices do we need to examine through the lens of equity or cultural competency?
- How are we translating our learning and knowledge into actions and application?
- Are we missing anything? If so, what?

In Pairs Only:

- What comments resonated with you, and why?
- What do staff members at Ferdinand understand, and what do they not understand?
- What do you understand, and what do you not understand?

In Your Personal Journal:

- Did you recognize any biases you might have, which were expressed by characters in this scenario? If so, what were they and where did you learn them? If not, did you recognize them in someone you know? Where might they have learned them?
- How might your cultural identity be influencing your perceptions, behaviors, and decision making?
- How can you better translate your knowledge and learning in cultural competency training into behavioral changes that positively influence student outcomes?
- Using an identity development model, the culturally proficient framework, or the Cultural Competency Continuum, assess where you are in your development of cultural competency skills.

Key Takeaways:

- Cultural competency is not a spectator learning activity. You must translate that learning into actions and applications. It's not merely a body of knowledge. It's a way of being. It's a way of professional practice. And it must be an ongoing process of reflection, critique, and personal challenge.
- Learning to be culturally competent means examining deeply held beliefs and values that may be so embedded in your cultural context that you may rarely examine them and hardly ever challenge or critique them.
- Talking about issues related to equitable education and access for all students is an ongoing process.

Exercise 34 Handout: "Fatigue at Ferdinand High" Scenario

Characters:
Cathy, counselor
Wendy, math teacher
Andy, art teacher
Yousef, JROTC instructor

Cathy, Andy, and Yousef are in the lunchroom having a robust debate about *Dancing with the Stars*. This is Yousef's first year of teaching, and all his colleagues have been warm, accepting, and inclusive, making him feel right at home. A few of them have even sought his advice on instructional issues. A gust of pride spreads across his lips and curves into a smile. Ferdinand could very well become his long-term professional home.

Yousef has had some challenges as any first-year teacher might, but nothing he hasn't been able to handle. He's hoping today will not be the exception because what began as a normal lunch conversation shifted when Wendy walked in the room. Trudging into the lunchroom, she threw a burrito in the microwave. From the look on her face, she is clearly upset, if not enraged. Yousef doesn't know her well, but he's never seen her quite this way before. Despite his best instincts, he speaks up first: "Wendy, is everything OK?"

Wendy: [Shaking her head] These kids are driving me crazy!

Yousef: Wendy, you gotta stop letting these kids get to you. Have you seen the way most of them live? Heck, if I lived in some of the places these kids do, I'd be angry too. What did they do today?

Wendy: Well, today Roberto strolls into class five minutes late. No tardy slip, nothing. He just strolls in and takes his seat like he owns the place. When I remind him that he needs to bring a tardy slip, he mumbles some stupid excuse and puts his head down.

Andy: What was his excuse?

Wendy: He said that he had to take care of something and that he got here as soon as he could. That's no excuse. That's the same reason *everybody* is late. So I tell him to go to the front office because I am not about to interrupt my class to argue about this.

Cathy: [Scoffs] Sounds like you already did.

Yousef: But he left the room, right?

Wendy: Yeah, but not before calling me a heartless bitch and slamming the door.

Andy: That's verbal abuse. You should have called Officer Ginsberg. He body-slammed the last kid who called me a name. Bam! Right up against a concrete wall. I've had no problem since then.

Cathy: I would have called his mother.

Wendy: I would—if he had one. He's being raised by his grandmother and, frankly, I think she can hardly handle him herself. She looks exhausted every time I see her, and all she does is plead with him to behave and listen to his teachers. It's a waste of time.

Yousef: I know what you mean. Most of these kids don't have fathers at home. Without positive role models, it's no wonder they struggle in school.

Wendy: Wait, it gets worse. After Roberto leaves, Fatimah jumps up in the middle of class and accuses me of being unfair.

Andy: [Looking surprised.] Fatimah? The girl with the long braids? She hardly ever says anything.

Wendy: That's the one. You know, her hair smells funny to me.

Cathy: I don't understand why we even allow that. There ought to be something in our dress code that prevents kids from wearing braids.

Yousef: There were women in my service unit who wore braids. Never bothered me.

Wendy: Well, it bothers me. Anyway, I threw her out the room, too, for being disruptive and disrespectful.

Andy: Then what?

Wendy: Then Gary jumps up in the middle of class, gives me a middle finger, and tells me that I don't understand what is really going on.

Cathy: I guess you threw him out, too.

Wendy: No, no. I told him to sit down and that we'd talk about it later. I know his mother. She teaches at Emerson. He's a good kid overall. Something must have upset him. Besides, he's one of the few students in that class who really deserves to be there. Half the class has huge gaps in their learning that prevent them from grasping many of the concepts needed to understand calculus. There was a time when most of those kids would be in special ed or remedial math. Now everybody's supposed to be college ready, even when they don't want to be and obviously aren't prepared to be.

Yousef: So, were you finally able to get on with your lesson?

Wendy: That's the thing. More than halfway through the period, Roberto and Fatimah come waltzing back into class with a note from Ms. Johnson asking me to sit down with them and discuss the problem they are having. Who's got time for that? I'm trying to teach a class! I'm so frustrated. We get no support from administration around here. And every time we say something, they direct us to learning about cultural competency.

Andy: Oh, if I hear another word about cultural competency, I'm going to puke. I'm so tired of talking about race and racism and equity ad nauseum. It's like everything is my fault and that I'm to blame for being who I am.

Wendy: I know. My parents worked hard for everything they got, but I'm supposed to feel bad about it. We need a break. We can't be responsible for all the problems people face in the world.

Cathy: I mean it's good information and all that, but what does cultural competency have to do with anything that has happened here today? I think we've had enough training on this. It's time to talk about something else!

[Andy, Wendy, and Cathy turn to look at Yousef. Andy speaks for all three of them.]

Andy: You understand where we're coming from Yousef, don't you?

As Quarter 2 Draws to a Close . . .

In this second quarter of the school year, we have focused on cultural competency in our professional practice. We began by examining the empirically supported tenets of culturally responsive teaching, explored the contributions of various U.S. citizens and how or if they are included in curriculum, analyzed our practices in discipline and cultural messages, and practiced designing our own culturally responsive lessons.

Take a moment to review the "Apply and Act" section of the Cultural Competency Continuum to self-evaluate your growth in cultural competency (see Figure 5.1). You may not yet feel proficient in all areas, but take the time to celebrate your areas of growth and understanding. We're halfway there!

Figure 5.1 **Apply and Act**

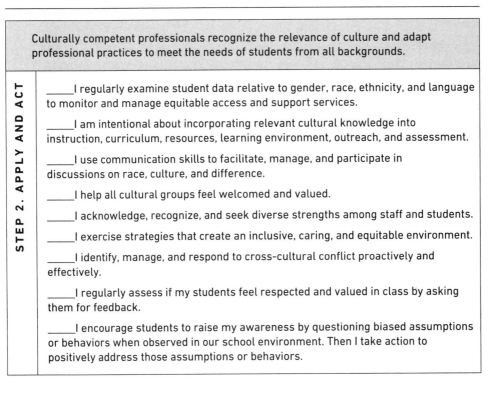

Culturally competent professionals recognize the relevance of culture and adapt professional practices to meet the needs of students from all backgrounds.

STEP 2. APPLY AND ACT

_____I regularly examine student data relative to gender, race, ethnicity, and language to monitor and manage equitable access and support services.

_____I am intentional about incorporating relevant cultural knowledge into instruction, curriculum, resources, learning environment, outreach, and assessment.

_____I use communication skills to facilitate, manage, and participate in discussions on race, culture, and difference.

_____I help all cultural groups feel welcomed and valued.

_____I acknowledge, recognize, and seek diverse strengths among staff and students.

_____I exercise strategies that create an inclusive, caring, and equitable environment.

_____I identify, manage, and respond to cross-cultural conflict proactively and effectively.

_____I regularly assess if my students feel respected and valued in class by asking them for feedback.

_____I encourage students to raise my awareness by questioning biased assumptions or behaviors when observed in our school environment. Then I take action to positively address those assumptions or behaviors.

6

Analyze and Align

Last quarter we focused on classroom practices. This quarter, we will broaden our focus to the school as an institution. We will examine policies, procedures, and practices in our school for possible privilege or bias, dismantle those that are, and sharpen our skills in confronting racism and managing conflict.

The exercises that we will be completing this quarter are heavily reliant on data from your schools and districts. Start hunting down the school improvement plan; teacher, student, and parent handbooks; teacher, student, and parent codes of conduct; and any other crucial policy materials that inform your day-to-day practices schoolwide. We're about to play a critical game of hide-and-seek, where we look for hidden forms of bias and privilege embedded in the school culture, policies, and practices. And then we'll practice what to do if we find them. It's a little more complicated than yelling, "Olly, olly, oxen, free"—calling to things hidden to come out in the open. We'll have to go looking for them, disrupting cultural icons and attitudes that may be dusty and outdated. But by the end of this quarter, you should feel more comfortable identifying the educational nooks and crannies where inequity can sometimes hide and confronting it systematically and professionally.

Exercises for Quarter 3

Following are 12 exercises that will help you *analyze and align* the policies, procedures, and practices in your school to prevent or eliminate possible privilege or bias.

Exercise 35: Pride and Prejudice

Time: 20 minutes

Materials: Exercise 35 homework handout (see p. 200)

Learning Objective: To explore an appreciation for our multiple identities and those of others

Facilitator Guidelines:

1. Tell participants they will be called on, in each of the three rounds, to organize themselves by the different identities they embrace (e.g., racial identity, gender identity, religious identity). Point out the four corners of the room as obvious choices for them to gather, although they will be responsible for organizing themselves.

2. Announce Round 1. Tell participants they have five minutes to organize *by racial identity*, a socially constructed category that may shift over time. (I purposefully do not provide the racial categories to allow people to self-identify.) Those with multiple racial identities are to go to the group with which they most closely identify. Participants will discuss two questions:

   ► What do you love or appreciate about this identity?

   ► What do you love or appreciate about the other identities in the room?

3. Announce Round 2. Tell participants they have five minutes to organize *by gender identity* to discuss two questions:

   ► What do you love or appreciate about this identity?

   ► What do you love or appreciate about the other identities in the room?

4. Announce Round 3. Participants have five minutes to organize *by religious identity* to discuss two questions:

   ► What do you love or appreciate about this identity?

   ► What do you love or appreciate about the other identities in the room?

Whole-Group Discussion:

• We all have multiple identities. Why do some people experience discomfort or fear when groups with common identities or experiences organize?

- When do groups with common identities become legitimately threatening to others?
- When do groups with common identities or experiences benefit from organizing?
- What would a group with a common identity (such as educators who unite to dismantle inequitable practices in schools) love and appreciate about this common identity? Together, how can this identity become one of the most fulfilling and purposeful identities we have? How will we know when or if we achieved this identity together?
- As a group of people organized to eliminate inequity, what would you like to call yourselves? Who are we collectively when we are culturally competent? How would we categorize ourselves (e.g., equity warriors, antiracist activists, culturally competent educators, social justice advocates)?

Key Takeaways:
- If you love and appreciate your own multiple identities, you can learn to love and appreciate others' identities.
- Organizing with people with similar identities or experiences can be a healthy and supportive endeavor.
- When groups with common identities or experiences organize to hurt, harm, or hate other people or identities, it is legitimately reasonable for people to feel threatened or fearful. It is also an emotionally unhealthy environment for all identities and can create a "hostile environment" in legal terms.
- You can craft characteristics and traits for a common identity. You can share common pride in this identity. You can have common experiences you share in this work. And it may be one of the most fulfilling identities you have!

Homework: Read "White Fatigue: Naming the Challenge in Moving from an Individual to a Systemic Understanding of Racism" by Joseph E. Flynn Jr. (2015). Discuss with your learning partner using the questions in the Exercise 35 homework handout.

Exercise 36: But for Barriers
Time: 45 minutes
Materials: Master schedule, Exercise 36 handout
Learning Objective: To identify potential barriers to school programs and strategize how to eliminate them

Facilitator Guidelines:

1. Have participants read the scenario "But for Barriers." In groups of four to five, participants should make a list of the programs available at their school to support students. Beside each offering, they should analyze whether any limitations or barriers exist that would prevent a student from accessing the programs.

2. If barriers are found, brainstorm how the program might be modified to increase student access.

Homework: Share your list of the programs available at your school with students. Let them complete the "I Have a Question" portion of the listing, if appropriate. Determine whether there are programs or services students would like to access but haven't, as well as their reasons for not accessing them. Discuss your findings with your learning partner and strategize how to resolve any barriers.

Exercise 36 Handout: "But for Barriers" Scenario

Justin Middle School had a reputation for being one of the most prestigious public schools in the district. Students at this school transitioned to the best college preparatory schools in the state. There was a waiting list, of course, but only the students with the best achievement scores stood a chance.

To the Roberts family's delight, little Marvin Roberts made the cut! They sat down immediately to review the vast services now at Marvin's disposal. Here is a list of the questions they had regarding access to those services.

Roberts Family Questions

Programs Available	Interest (Yes or No)	I Have a Question
Advanced Placement Classes	Yes!	Requires referral by counselor. I've been trying to reach him. What should I do next?
After-School Tutoring	Yes!	I need to ride public transportation home. If I do this, will I be able to get home before dark?
Extracurricular Sports	Yes!	We don't have the money for the athletic exam and additional fees. Can you waive these?
Field Trips	Yes!	Do these cost money?
Business Club	Yes!	This club requires a prerequisite accounting class, but that wasn't offered in my last school.
Engineering Camp	Yes!	This looks like it is held at the university 50 miles away. How will I get there?
Photography Club	Yes!	Does it matter how old the camera is?
Yoga Class	Yes!	This starts before I arrive at school.
Parent Advisory Team	Yes!	My mom works during the day. Are any meetings scheduled in the evening?

After reviewing Marvin's questions, the staff determined that although they had numerous school offerings for students, not all students could access them easily. They had some planning to do to accommodate everyone.

Exercise 37: Equal vs. Equitable

Time: 60 minutes (you may choose to do the analysis portions in more than one session as there are seven programmatic areas to review)

Materials: Five school T-shirts (three size mediums, one size small, and one size large or extra-large), seven tables with large butcher sheets and markers for debriefing

Learning Objective: To examine the difference between equal and equitable

Facilitator Guidelines:

1. Ask for volunteers from the participants. Select three volunteers of varying physical size: one small, one medium, and one large. Tell them they will each receive a T-shirt and to be perfectly fair, each person will receive the same size.

2. Distribute the three size medium T-shirts to the three volunteers. Ask them to put the shirt on over their outfit so others can see how it fits. If you have selected your volunteers wisely, one person will have a T-shirt that is too large and another will have one that is too small.

3. Ask each of the volunteers if they like the way their T-shirt fits.

4. Ask them if they believe you were fair in how you distributed the shirts.

5. Explain that you desired to make everything as equal as possible, so each was given the same size shirt, regardless of their body type. This is *equality*. Everyone gets the same thing regardless of who they are, and this is what it means to be equal.

6. Ask them if there is a better way to make sure each person receives a T-shirt that meets their needs.

7. Now distribute the correct size for each volunteer, and ask them to replace the one they are wearing with this one.

8. Ask them again if they like the way the T-shirt fits now.

9. Ask them again if they believe you were fair in how you distributed these T-shirts.

10. Ask them again if it is fair to provide each person with exactly what they need. This is *equity*, and this is what it means to be equitable.

Small-Group Debrief: Place one topic at each of the seven tables. People can wander from table to table and write their comments on a butcher sheet provided.

- Examine our athletic program. What practices are equal? What practices are equitable? Are they fair for all?

- Examine our music program. What practices are equal? What practices are equitable? Are they fair for all?

- Examine our gifted/advanced placement program. What practices are equal? What practices are equitable? Are they fair for all?
- Examine our lunch program. What practices are equal? What practices are equitable? Are they fair for all?
- Examine our library program. What practices are equal? What practices are equitable? Are they fair for all?
- Examine our professional development program. What practices are equal? What practices are equitable? Are they fair for all?
- Examine our hiring practices. What practices are equal? What practices are equitable? Are they fair for all?

Whole-Group Debrief: What changes need to be made, and how do we hold ourselves accountable for doing it?

Key Takeaways:

- Equality is not always fair if someone needs more than another person to have a successful "fit." We are all different and have different needs.
- Being equitable may mean that some people get more and some people get less, but it is still fair if everyone gets what they need.

Homework: In your personal journals, examine your personal instructional, assessment, and classroom management approaches. What practices are equal? What practices are equitable? Are they fair for all? Discuss with your learning partner.

Exercise 38: Race to Equity

Time: 20 minutes

Materials: 15 heavy books, a long hallway with no student interruptions

Learning Objective: To examine the difference between equality and equity

Facilitator Guidelines:

1. Ask for three volunteers, and take them into the school hallway. (You must do this when students are not likely to be there. The rest of the staff may line the hallways.)
2. Tell the three volunteers they are going to race from one end of the hallway to the other. Assign another volunteer to stand at the end of the hallway so they can flag the winner when the runner crosses the finish line.
3. Have the three volunteers line up equally, but give one volunteer 5 heavy books to carry and another volunteer 10 heavy books to carry during the race.
4. Inform the volunteers that the race will begin in staggered starts of 10 seconds and to watch for your signal. When you give the first signal, have the runner with no books start. Ten seconds later, signal the runner

with five books to start. Finally, after another 10 seconds, signal the third runner with 10 books to start.

5. Ask the other staff members to cheer on the runners because, theoretically, they each have an equal chance of winning the race.

6. At the finish line, award the winner a gift, praising them for their brilliance and ingenuity.

Whole-Group Debrief:

- Was each runner given an equal chance of winning the race? Why or why not?

- What would have made the race more equitable?

- This race is a metaphor for the challenges people of color have historically faced economically. What kinds of "books" have they had to carry?

- This race had staggered starts. Within our history, who got a head start on building wealth, social capital, educational opportunities, and the full rights of citizenry? How did they do that? Who got the late starts, and why? When were the educational opportunities and full citizenry rights granted to marginalized populations? What evidence supports that they have those rights today? What evidence suggests they have yet to be fulfilled?

- What kinds of practices, policies, programs, or procedures might help support students who have been historically marginalized?

- Which ones do we currently have in place, and which ones do we need to create?

- What are our specific targets, and how do we hold each other accountable for achieving them?

Key Takeaways:

- We were well into the 20th century (1954) when the Supreme Court allowed children of color to attend schools that had previously denied their entrance—usually ones with high-quality books, facilities, and resources. We were even further into the 20th century when it was established that people of color could vote without harassment, imprisonment, or undue barriers to prevent it. That law remains fiercely challenged to this day.

- In addition to getting a late start, people of color had to overcome numerous barriers that were established to prohibit their entry into society: the restriction of job opportunities and residential neighborhoods; predatory rates for insurance, loans, housing, and banking; inferior schools and resources; limiting income; insecure job status—you name it, there was a Jim Crow law to reinforce white supremacy.

- The fact that so many people of color overcame these barriers to transcend into middle or upper class is a tribute to their hard work, ingenuity, and tenacity. The fact that so many people of color have been unable to over-come these barriers speaks to the onerous socioeconomic weights some have had to endure along with the late starts and the need for supports to catch up.

Exercise 39: The Joy of Codependency

Time: 20 minutes

Materials: Duct tape, outdoor space or gym, sneakers or athletic shoes for participants, water bottles, smartphone

Learning Objective: To explore the codependency of teachers and students in the learning process

Facilitator Guidelines:

1. Divide staff into teams of two; each player must assume the role of Player A or Player B.

2. Ask team members to use the duct tape to strap one of their legs to that of their partner. When complete, each person will have one leg free and one leg taped to their partner's leg.

3. Have sets of five or six teams compete to complete a set of tasks together. Choose between five to eight tasks from the list below.

Possible Team Tasks

- Step through a series of hula hoops.
- Do 10 squats.
- Do 5 bunny hops.
- Walk 10 steps in a high knee walk.
- Do 5 lunges.
- Hold a Downward Dog yoga pose for 30 seconds.
- Dance the Twist for 30 seconds.
- Go up or down a set of steps.
- Do 5 leg lifts lying on your back.
- Sit down together.
- Do 10 sit-ups.
- Make 3 free throws.
- Play a short (60-second) game of Twister.
- Throw a Frisbee and retrieve it.

4. After each set of teams has completed their tasks, partners may unwrap the duct tape and face each other. Player A must now decide two tasks for Player B to complete on his or her own. They can be tasks they completed

together or two completely different tasks. Both tasks must be completed within two minutes. Whatever task Player A requests, Player B must make every effort to complete.

Whole-Group Debrief:

- Rate your team's effectiveness to complete the tasks together on a scale of 1 to 10; justify your score to each other.
- What challenges did you overcome together, and how did you do that?
- What was the role of failure in completing the tasks together?
- In the second part of our activity, one person became responsible for determining the tasks of their partner. Player As, how, if at all, did the first set of tasks prepare you for deciding the tasks you wanted your partner to complete?
- What parallels can you make between these activities today and your work with students every day? In what way might your students eventually assume a predominant role in deciding things that affect you personally?
- What kinds of practices, policies, procedures, or programs would create an environment in which teacher and student interdependency was made explicit?

Key Takeaways:

- Your destiny, in many ways, is connected to the lives you teach and influence.
- Your students' success or failures shape their perceptions and world view.
- Someday, as part of the voting public, your students will be responsible for making decisions that may directly affect you, your family, or your environment. Teach them well—*all of them*. They are your future society.
- Using your smartphone, read Dorothy Nolte's famous poem, "Children Learn What They Live" before discussing the next question: What kind of a world are you shaping every day in your interactions, practices, programs, and policies with all students?

Exercise 40: Conflict Cards

Time: 20 minutes

Materials: Index cards, Exercise 40 handout

Learning Objective: To examine how we resolve conflicts in groups

Facilitator Guidelines:

1. Have participants form groups of four, and distribute the Exercise 40 handout to them.

2. Team members should cut out the name cards and place them in the center of the table. Use one list or multiple lists, depending on the number of groups.

3. Ask each group to categorize the names on the basis of *personal characteristics or traits*. Remember, categorizing by race, gender, or profession is excluded. There is but one nonnegotiable: Everyone in the group must agree on the categories and on where the names are placed. Provide at least 10 minutes for this activity.

Small-Group Debrief:

- What made this task difficult?
- How did your group resolve any conflicts?
- What skills did you use to resolve conflict?
- What worked well, and what didn't?
- If someone in your group made a comment you found offensive, take the next five minutes to share respectfully what they said and why it offended you. If you are confronted by someone, take this time to listen, reflect, and respond with respect.
- Based on your experience in this activity and your collective life experiences, craft a group statement of your Top 10 Tips for Resolving Conflict. Record them on an index card. You will be asked to share these in the larger group.

Whole-Group Debrief:

- Listen to the tips from each team.
- Which of these tips, if any, should be standard practice for all staff?
- How would you institutionalize them?

Homework: Have each team assign someone to post their team's tips online. (An Excel spreadsheet works well for this.) Each participant should then review all the tips and place an X beside the 10 tips they believe are the most important.

Exercise 40 Handout: Name Lists

Name List 1

Lin-Manuel Miranda	Caitlyn Jenner	Michael Cohen	Britney Spears	Cardi B
Deb Haaland	Cher	Meghan Markle	Crown Prince Mohammed bin Salman	Colin Kaepernick
Issa Rae	Trevor Noah	Kathy Griffin	O.J. Simpson	Roseanne Barr
Sean Hannity	Jennifer Lopez	Rihanna	Ronan Farrow	Maxine Waters

Name List 2

Oprah Winfrey	Jeff Bezos	Elon Musk	Fidel Castro	Winston Churchill
Tiffany Haddish	Priyanka Chopra	Charlize Theron	Julia-Louis Dreyfus	Ta-Nehisi Coates
Ted Bundy	Ariana Grande	George W. Bush	Taraji P. Henson	Franklin D. Roosevelt
Adolf Hitler	Martin Luther King Jr.	Alexandria Ocasio-Cortez	Angela Merkel	Tiger Woods

Name List 3

Reince Priebus	Malia Obama	Chelsea Clinton	James Comey	Malcolm X
Kim Kardashian	Lester Holt	Betsy DeVos	Vladimir Putin	Kim Jong-Un
Nelson Mandela	Mahatma Gandhi	Bill Cosby	Kevin Spacey	George Zimmerman
Kirstjen Nielsen	Nicki Minaj	Dwayne Johnson	Pope Francis	Mark Zuckerberg

Exercise 41: Conflict Partners

Time: 20 minutes

Materials: Online data from the Top 10 Tips spreadsheet, Exercise 41 handouts 1 and 2

Learning Objective: To examine how we resolve conflicts in groups

Facilitator Guidelines:

1. Using the data from the online compilation of tips, formulate the collective Top 10 Tips for Resolving Conflict as determined by participant votes. Post for all participants to refer to.

2. Ask participants to test the Top 10 Tips in today's activity. They will be asked to assess their efficacy at the end of the exercise.

3. Ask participants to get into pairs and face each other. Give one partner the Exercise 41 handout 1 ("Calvin's Story") and the other partner the Exercise 41 handout 2 ("Miss Cindy's Story"). One partner will play the role of Calvin, and the other partner will play the role of Miss Cindy. Ask each partner to read their scenario before beginning their dialogue. Provide at least 10 minutes for this activity.

Partner Debrief: Calvins, critique your Miss Cindys. Exchange handouts so you both understand the challenges you faced.

- What did they do well? In what areas might they improve?
- Review the conflict resolution skills used during your interaction. Which ones worked well, and which ones did not? How would each of you modify your toolbox?
- What kinds of policies, procedures, or programs (or lack of them) might have created an environment in which this scenario occurred?

Homework: Based on your experience today, modify the 10 tips to individualize your approach to solving conflict. Ensure the tips include what works especially well for you.

Exercise 41 Handout 1: Calvin's Story

Today you're Calvin, a student at Avery Tristan Elementary School. This morning you didn't complete your writing assignment. And why should you? You've got too many more important things on your mind. Last night your house caught fire, and you had to stand outside in the cold until your grandmother came to get you, your mother, and your siblings.

You have no idea what's ahead for you or your family. You only have the clothes on your back that you wore to school yesterday—and if anybody says anything about it, you're angry enough to punch them. Breakfast this morning was a hurried slice of toast and a glass of milk. Grandma hadn't planned on company. Mom insisted you go to school because she will have a lot of running around to do today to secure housing. But before she dropped you off at school, she warned you to *not* tell your business to your teacher, Miss Cindy. She doesn't want any nosy counselors or social workers sniffing around; she warned you they might attempt to take you away from her.

Look at your teacher, Miss Cindy. Little Miss Perfect Life. She looks as though she doesn't have a care in the world. What does she know about hardships? She would burst into tears if she broke a fingernail! Anyway, she is making you go to lunch late to give you more time to work on your assignment. You are hungry. You are irritable. You are tired. You are frustrated. You are scared. And you feel like nobody cares.

So the last thing you're going to do is write this assignment. Only now, Miss Cindy wants to talk about it. Keep your chin up. Don't tell her anything if you want to stay with your mom. Your goal is to avoid squealing about your family's situation and hurry her up so you can go to lunch. Let's get this over with. Sure, you'll talk with Miss Cindy, but you'll let her go first. Then you'll wipe that confident smug smile right off her face and give her conflict resolution skills a robust test drive!

Exercise 41 Handout 2: Miss Cindy's Story

Today you're Miss Cindy, a teacher at Avery Tristan Elementary School. This morning your student, Calvin, didn't complete his writing assignment. He's perfectly capable of doing this assignment, but his mother warned you that he can be very stubborn and dig in his heels when he chooses. She wants you to take a hard line with him and hold him accountable to the same expectations you have for everyone else. She has high hopes for him—and so do you. Failure is not an option!

You've been earnestly trying to make inroads in building a relationship with Calvin, but he usually seems distant, unmotivated, and disinterested in anything related to school. You asked him to stay after class for 10 minutes before he goes to lunch so he can have some extra time to complete the assignment. Yet instead of working, he put his head down on his desk and folded his arms. How are you supposed to teach someone who refuses to learn? Apparently, he doesn't care about being late to lunch either!

Your goal is to motivate him to complete the assignment. How you're going to do that will take your best communication skills. You asked him to talk with you for a moment. He looks reluctant. Take a deep breath and remain patient. Maybe he can at least get started in the next few minutes. Begin a conversation with Calvin to achieve your goal, and let's give those conflict resolution skills you chose a real test drive!

Exercise 42: A Very Barry Conflict

Time: 45 minutes

Materials: Exercise 42 handouts 1 and 2, participants' revised Top 10 Tips for Conflict Resolution

Learning Objective: To practice confronting racist language or acts

Facilitator Guidelines:

1. Pass out the Exercise 42 handout 1, "How to Confront a Racist Comment or Act." Ask participants to read and discuss the handout in pairs. They have 15 minutes.

2. Next pass out the Exercise 42 handout 2, "A Very Barry Conflict." Ask participants to read the scenario independently and then practice with their partner how they would respond, using the Exercise 42 handout 1, as well as their personalized Top 10 Tips for Conflict Resolution.

3. Follow up with a debrief.

Partner Debrief:

Critique your partner's skills in confronting your words and actions. What did they do well, and how might they improve?

Whole-Group Debrief:

- What made this conversation difficult, if anything, and what did you do to overcome that difficulty?
- What skills or strategies did you find helpful in having this conversation?
- What would you do differently?
- Should this incident be documented or reported? Why or why not?
- What might create an environment in which this incident could happen?
- What kinds of programs, policies, or procedures would help Barry be successful in this school or wherever he goes?
- What are your next steps to support and protect Barry?

Homework: Read "Law and Policy on the Concept of Bullying at School" by Dewey Cornell and Susan P. Limber (2015). Be prepared to teach the article to the staff at the next meeting; teams will be randomly selected to do so.

Exercise 42 Handout 1: How to Confront a Racist Comment or Act

One of the most difficult things to do as an equity warrior is to confront someone who makes a comment or commits an act that is offensive, hurtful, or oppressive to others. But you wouldn't stand by and let someone bully another person, would you? Here are some ways you can confront someone who intentionally or unintentionally is hurting you or others with their words or actions.

1. **Remain calm and safe.** Always be in control of your emotions, and don't allow anyone to trigger your anger. If you lose control, you may fail to be heard and risk losing credibility as a voice of reason and a scholar of the movement to reduce bias and injustice. Refrain from calling names or hurling labels. Let the other person's behavior or words speak for themselves. Also, scan your environment to make sure you and others are safe. If you don't feel physically safe, use your facial expression to convey disapproval or disagreement but leave immediately and encourage anyone else who may be at risk to leave as well.

2. **Ask a critical question.** Sometimes the best response is asking a question that makes a person pause and think. These are essentially the same kinds of critical questions you design for students when you're teaching a complex topic. Here are some examples:
   - Why do you think that is funny?
   - Do you believe that statement applies to everyone? Why or why not?
   - What might be the long-term implications of your actions?
   - Why does that bother you?
   - How do you justify that action as respectful? And if you can't justify it, why would you do or say that?
   - Would you find it offensive if someone said that to you or your child?

3. **Articulate how the words or actions affect you or others.** Articulate how what was said or done is hurtful, biased, disrespectful, or oppressive toward a target. The perpetrator may not even be aware of how their words or actions are affecting others. Assume positive intentionality, and remind them that *how* they say things is as important as what they say. If something they have said is false, courageously call it so. Question the fairness or justice of their words, actions, or the issues they raise—not the person or their character. You cannot prove intent or quality of character, but actions and words speak volumes. Hold the person accountable to those.

4. **Express empathy for the target or share lived experiences.** People get frustrated or upset and want to be heard, but whatever they say, they

can say with kindness, respect, and preservation of others' dignity. Let the person know that you heard what they said and that you acknowledge the feelings they expressed, but redirect them to how their words or actions are being negatively experienced by others. Chances are good that the person saying or doing hurtful things to others cannot or has not seen themselves in the target. They have not stopped to imagine what their target's life is like and how their humanity intersects with others in real and meaningful ways. Ask them to imagine what it might be like to walk in the target's shoes. Encourage them to get to know people individually and share positive lived experiences that relate to the issues raised. Offer to provide data or research to support your experiences.

5. **Appeal to shared values.** If you know the person who has made what you deem a disrespectful comment, joke, or taunt, connect with them on a value you believe you share with them: "Mary, I've always known you to be a fair person, but your comments today don't reflect that." Disclose your own values and why their words or actions conflict with those values. Let the person know that what they said or did is creating distance between you and them, based on your values. Discuss with them why you see things differently and what values you acted on to make that decision.

6. **Do, document, and report.** Do something. You may not change the mind of the person or influence their actions, but don't allow another generation of students to be subjugated, terrorized, marginalized, or maligned, with you sitting on the sidelines afraid to speak up. Understand that everyone is not ready to change or may be at different places in their identity development, but they may well remember the voice that made them pause, even if they didn't choose to follow it. And if you choose to say nothing, they will also consider your silence as complicit with their behavior. If you feel threatened, walk away, but document the incident and report it to someone who should be able to help. Be a role model to give others the courage to speak up when they see injustice, and distance yourself from those who persist in perpetuating harm to others, despite your objections.

Exercise 42 Handout 2: A Very Barry Conflict

It's a seemingly normal school afternoon. Your students have just been dismissed to go to their electives when suddenly you hear a loud sound, like a truck hitting the wall, in the hallway. The sound is followed by the squeals and shouts of young voices.

"What's all that ruckus about?" you ask yourself, venturing outside the door. That's when you see Tom, the teacher next door, shaking his finger at a young boy, whom you recognize as Barry. Tom barrels his face practically nose to nose with Barry. "Tom!" you exclaim. "What in the world is going on?"

"Somebody stole my lunch!" Tom is livid. "I know he did it, but I can't hardly understand anything he is saying! We got all these kids from everywhere! You come to this country, you learn English, comprende?" Barry ducks and scrambles away running down the hallway.

"Tom, why don't you come in my room?" you offer. Tom obliges, and the other students disperse. Barry is one of only a handful of students of color in the school. He was quickly labeled a troublemaker by some of the staff, although he's always helpful and attentive in your class. Alone with Tom behind closed doors you feel the need to have a conversation about bias, equity, and respect.

Turn to your partner, and have this conversation with them as though they were Tom. Refer to the handout when needed, then each of you swap roles.

Exercise 43: Teacher, Teacher, I Declare

Time: 60 minutes

Materials: Homework article from Exercise 42 ("Law and Policy on the Concept of Bullying at School"); a copy of the district policy on bullying or harassment; a copy of the school handbook section on bullying or harassment

Learning Objective: To learn the legal aspects of bullying, harassment, and fostering a hostile environment

Facilitator Guidelines:

1. Place the names of all the learning partners in a basket.

2. Randomly select 12 teams from the basket. Each team will describe one of the 12 sections of the reading, "Law and Policy on the Concept of Bullying at School."

Team 1: Introduce the article and discuss why bullying in schools is an important societal issue.

Team 2: Conceptual Challenges: Discuss this section and facilitate whole-group dialogue on the following questions:

- What do the authors define as bullying?
- How do the authors define racism?
- What are the similarities and differences?

Team 3: Civil Rights and Bullying: Discuss this section and facilitate whole-group dialogue on the following questions:

- What is harassment?
- How does it relate to racism?

Team 4: Federal Guidance on Bullying and Harassment: Discuss this section with staff.

Team 5: State Laws on Bullying and *Key Provisions in State Bullying Laws:* Discuss these two sections with staff.

Team 6: Reporting Incidents of Bullying and *Disciplinary Policies:* Discuss these two sections with staff.

Team 7: Prevention and Support Services: Discuss this section with staff.

Team 8: Statutory Definitions of Bullying: Discuss this section with staff.

Team 9: Challenges of Conflating Harassment and Bullying in State Law: Discuss this section with staff.

Team 10: Challenges of Conflating Bullying with Other Peer Aggression in State Law: Discuss this section with staff.

Team 11: Bullying Within State Criminal Laws: Discuss this section with staff.

Team 12: Recommendations: Discuss this section with staff.

Homework:

- Be on heightened awareness for signs of bullying or harassment in the school environment.
- Be particularly diligent in observing how students of difference are treated by other students and staff in the school.
- Discuss your findings with your learning partner.

Exercise 44: Tripod of a Hostile Environment: Bullying, Harassment, and Racism

Time: 60 minutes

Materials: A copy of the district policy on bullying or harassment, a copy of the school handbook section on bullying or harassment (participants need their own copies of both documents)

Learning Objective: To learn the legal aspects of bullying and fostering a hostile environment

Facilitator Guidelines:

1. Divide into groups of four to five to review the district policy on bullying, harassment, civil rights, or acts of racism.
2. If there is a student or parent handbook on school policies, have participants review those as well.
3. Follow up with small-group debrief questions.

Small-Group Debrief:

- Discuss your observations within the school environment this week. What did you learn about bullying or harassment in the school when you focused on it?
- Do our practices align with our policies? Are our espoused values the same as our lived values?
- Are there any policies that advantage some groups of students and disadvantage others? Which ones are applied equally, and which ones are applied equitably?
- What is our legal responsibility in cases of bullying, harassment, or racism?
- What changes, if any, do we need to make in our practices or school policies to ensure all students are always treated with respect and dignity?
- What can we do better, and how do we hold ourselves accountable for doing it?

Whole-Group Debrief:
- Have each team summarize their discussion in their small groups.
- Where do we go from here?

Exercise 45: Eyes on the Ball!

Time: 40 minutes

Materials: Basketball court, basketball, participants in athletic wear and comfortable shoes (yes, you're going to play basketball!), Exercise 45 homework handout (see p. 201)

Learning Objective: To introduce colorism

Facilitator Guidelines:

1. Ask for 13 volunteers willing to play an eight-minute game of basketball: 10 players, 2 referees, and 1 scorekeeper/timeclock assistant. Designate 5 players for Team A and 5 for Team B.

2. For Team A only: *Discreetly* notify two of the players on this team that if their team receives the ball, they can only pass it between the two of them. They are not to pass the ball to the other three members on the team, and they are not to make those three team members, the spectators, or the referees aware of this rule.

3. Team B will start. Play ball!!

Whole-Group Debrief:
- How well did Team B work together? How could you tell?
- How well did Team A work together? How could you tell?
- Team A members, how did it feel to be on this team? Why?
- Why do you think anyone would ask a team member to exclude members of their own team from working together to win the game?

Analogy Reveal:

It's difficult to win a game against an opponent when members of the same team aren't working together. The offensive and defensive plays are crippled when team members hog the ball. Colonizers understood this and to cause disunity, they would often grant favors or privileges to some members of a given race, while denying them to others of the same race. The discriminating factor was skin color. Fairer-skinned people of a race were granted more privileges and opportunities than darker-skinned people within the same race. The result, which still exists today, is discrimination, bias, and racism within racial categories—a phenomena we call *colorism*.

Colorism might place someone in a position in which they are discriminated against by people outside of their race as well as by people *within* their own race, even though they are technically all on the same team! As we maintain a heightened awareness for harassment, bullying, and racism within schools, be aware that these can occur among students of the same race, a tainted legacy from our colonialized past.

Homework: Read "Everyday Colorism: Reading in the Language Arts Classroom" by Sarah L. Webb (2019). Discuss with your learning partner using the questions in the Exercise 45 homework handout.

Exercise 46: The Parable of the Farmers

Time: 20 minutes

Materials: Exercise 46 handout

Learning Objective: To analyze the role of equity advocate and ally and to strategize ways to be more effective

Facilitator Guidelines:

1. Have participants read "The Parable of the Farmers" scenario.
2. In small groups, have them discuss the parable, referring to the questions below.

Small-Group Debrief:

- What systems contributed to the continued plight of the valley farmers?
- How is confronting systemic or institutional racism different than confronting individual racism?
- What kinds of conflict did Leroy encounter?
- What strategies might he have used to confront racism more effectively?
- What did Leroy do that was effective? What did he do that was ineffective?
- What needs to happen in the mountain and valley communities, and how would you help bring about this change?

Exercise 46 Handout: "The Parable of the Farmers" Scenario

Newton County was a typical farming community, with farms that spread from the highest crests of majestic hilltops to the plains in the lower valley. It was a seemingly ideal place where people loved to live, learn, and work. Farmers talked about the crops. Farmers talked about the weather. They talked about drainage, erosion, football, families, and feed, but there was one topic that was too painful for many residents to broach.

Many years ago, the native mountain residents were forcefully removed from their land and relegated to lands in the valley. The mountain land was then redistributed to new farmers. The valley farmers protested these actions, but their objections were met with murderous threats and actions, courts that ignored their claims, and various forms of economic and social marginalization. Subsequently, the new mountain farmers routinely restricted the ability of valley residents to purchase farming supplies or equipment and limited their water supply.

And that's not all. Valley farmland had smaller acreages per plot and predatory interest rates. Smaller plots also meant fewer jobs and lower pay, so the farms and facilities fell into disrepair. The valley residents were left to grapple with internalized frustration as the new mountain farmers grew more and more oblivious to the implications of their actions on the valley farmers.

Except Leroy, who recognized vast disparities between the farms in the valley and those in the mountains. He could see that the mountain farmers benefitted from the actions of their predecessors, although they wouldn't dare endorse those kinds of predatory actions today. He observed that valley residents were treated differently in public spaces, and he refused to look away. As a mountain farmer, he chose to be a vocal ally for valley farmers and decided it was time to have a necessary conversation. However, he was ill-prepared for the response.

Some mountain farmers became quiet, distracted, or visually uncomfortable: "What are we talking about this for? How does this affect us?" Some attempted to change the subject: "Why aren't we talking about how valley farmers treat one another?" they demanded. When Leroy mentioned that the water resources intended to support farms in the valley had been diverted to mountain farms, the mountain farmers seemed unaware or disinterested. Some mountain farmers complained that he was making them uncomfortable and blaming them for a situation they did not create. Other mountain residents broke into tears and accused him of attacking them. They warned him about the valley farmers: "They are a dangerous and violent people!" They then showed him the films and videos they produced to support their position.

As things escalated, some mountain farmers grew enraged. They dismissed Leroy's inquiry as a waste of time. They couldn't understand how a collective structure of actions over time had placed the farmers in the valley in a cycle of oppression, inequitable outcomes, and disparate treatment. Even citizens who accepted the historical facts argued, "What's done is done. It's time for everyone to move on."

The mountain farmers' behavior deflected the glaring disparities of the community while maintaining a pattern of injustice they had the power to improve. Eventually Leroy's neighbors extinguished the necessary conversation. It. Was. Just. Too. Exhausting.

As Quarter 3 Draws to a Close . . .

We have explored a number of themes this quarter while we examined our schoolwide system for indicators of inequity and bias. We began to learn ways to confront racism proactively and positively. We were also introduced to an even more nuanced feature of racism: the bias and disparate outcomes that occur for darker skinned peoples within the same racial categories, families, and communities; among friends and neighbors; and in schools. What an insidious and unfair web of emotional pain these lies and false narratives have rendered across our entire society! There is much work to do, and no one is more equipped to do it than you!

Once again, it's time to take stock of your progress toward cultural competency. Review the "Analyze and Align" section of the Cultural Competency Continuum (see Figure 6.1). Check any statements with which you agree. Notice and celebrate your progress. Highlight those statements that you would like to learn more about. Check in with your learning partner to determine if the two of you are going to forge ahead together for the last quarter. Next up: Life in the fast lane—as an advocate and activist for equitable outcomes.

Figure 6.1 **Analyze and Align**

<table>
<tr>
<td rowspan="2" style="writing-mode:vertical-rl">STEP 3. ANALYZE AND ALIGN</td>
<td>Culturally competent professionals analyze policies, procedures, and programs that inhibit access and opportunity for historically marginalized students and staff and align resources to eradicate inequity in the school community.</td>
</tr>
<tr>
<td>

_____I know the legal issues surrounding racism, bullying, and fostering a hostile environment, and I examine policies and procedures to ensure my practices are fair and legally defensible.

_____I work with my colleagues to institutionalize our learning and implement agreed-on goals and vision.

_____I volunteer to work with colleagues in the selection of future personnel whose values align with the school's goals and vision—inclusive of increasing equity and access for students of color.

_____I volunteer to work with colleagues in aligning budgetary allocations with school goals and vision—inclusive of increasing equity and access for students of color.

_____I understand that my destiny is intertwined with the success or failure of all my students, and I work tirelessly to ensure that they are all successful.

_____I can effectively challenge racism, inequity, or discriminatory practices in a professional and proactive manner.

_____I own the responsibility for building an authentically inclusive and just classroom and school environment.

_____I empower parents to engage and lead.

_____I have critiqued various schoolwide policies and practices and worked to reduce or eliminate any that may perpetuate inequitable outcomes.

</td>
</tr>
</table>

7

Advocate and Lead

In this last quarter, we will hone our professional skills as leaders, advocates, and allies. We'll examine ways to connect with parents and community members, learn to facilitate discussions on race and equity, and sharpen our skills in advocacy for marginalized populations. These kinds of specialized leadership skills will prepare you for any additional roles you choose to pursue in education or in service to others. Most important, you will learn when to be silent and when to speak up. You will experience a gradual release of control in this quarter. The role of the facilitator will be reduced as you are asked to step up and take a greater leadership role in strategizing the resolution of issues. The critical questions after readings will be yours to create and facilitate. The examination of data and discussions will be yours to lead and navigate. And should you choose to speak up, this is the quarter where I hope you find your voice and empower others to find theirs. This is your time.

Exercises for Quarter 4

Following are 10 exercises that will support you as you *advocate and lead* in your new role as equity leader, advocate, and ally.

Exercise 47: The Rhetoric of Change

Time: 60 minutes

Materials: Exercise 47 handout

Learning Objective: To examine the lessons learned from one school that sought to improve parent engagement in a culturally diverse community

Facilitator Guidelines:

1. Ask participants to form small groups of four to five. Participants will read the article on parent involvement by sections in their small groups.

2. After each section, participants should respond to the following:

   ► Summarize what you read.

   ► What resonated with you, and why?

   ► What questions do you have, and how can you get them answered?

   ► What connections, if any, can you make to your work or practice?

Exercise 47 Handout: Parental Involvement

Read "Parental Involvement: Rhetoric of Inclusion in an Environment of Exclusion," by Allison A. Parsons, Katrina M. Walsemann, Sonya J. Jones, Herman Knopf, and Christine E. Blake (2018). Then discuss within your small groups the following questions.

- What kinds of changes made the school climate shift between the first and second buildings?

- Which policies were put into place without parent input? Why?

- What is the "rhetoric of colorblind racism?" Provide examples of how the staff demonstrated this.

- Why did the author equate assimilation with racism? Provide examples.

- Provide an example of deficit thinking and deficit language in a school setting. If someone thought that the way a minority child or parent did something was inferior to their ways of doing something, what would that comment sound like?

- SEP school had parent involvement policies, procedures, and practices, but those policies, procedures, and practices didn't seem to be building better relationships. Which ones needed to be examined? What needs to happen at this school to make it more inclusive and culturally responsive?

Exercise 48: The Parent Policy

Time: 30 minutes

Materials: Copies of the school's parent involvement policies from the district policy; parent handbook, student handbook, or teacher handbook

Learning Objective: To examine parental input into school policies that affect students

Facilitator Guidelines:

1. Ask participants to form groups of four to five.

2. Have them review the school's policies and discuss the following questions:

   ► To the best of your knowledge, which policies, if any, received significant parent input (e.g., student hairstyle regulations)? Which ones, if any, did not? Why?

   ► If there are policies that appear to not have received significant parent input, design a way to remedy this.

   ► Which parent involvement policies, practices, or procedures, if any, assume parental assimilation with the dominant culture (e.g., parent dress code)? How are the parental involvement policies, practices, or procedures consistent with the cultural values, beliefs, and practices of the school's parent population?

   ► Which parent involvement policies, practices, or procedures, if any, suggest deficit thinking or logic (e.g., punitive measures for parents)? In other words, do our parent involvement policies, practices, or procedures assume that parents or their children are in some way lacking and that our role is to "fix" them?

   ► What, in your opinion, needs to happen at the school to make it more inclusive and culturally responsive?

Exercise 49: The Advocate

Time: 30 minutes

Materials: Exercise 49 handout

Learning Objective: To examine the discreet skills of advocacy

Facilitator Guidelines:

1. Have participants divide into groups of four to five. Begin by referring to the last article participants read, "Parent Involvement: The Rhetoric of Inclusion in an Environment of Exclusion," by Allison A. Parsons, Katrina M. Walsemann, Sonya J. Jones, Herman Knopf, and Christine E. Blake (2018). Note that several parents at the SEP school (the school mentioned in the article) indicated they were afraid of the administrators.

Some disenrolled their children from the school without confronting the issues that made them unhappy.

2. All too often, when people are faced with situations they deem unfair, they don't feel equipped to confront the issues positively. They may need an advocate. If they asked you to help, where and how would you start?

3. Have participants read "Tips for Becoming a Fearless Equity Warrior" in the Exercise 49 handout and then discuss the tips in their groups. They have 10 minutes.

Small-Group Debrief:
- What are the risks of being an advocate in a system, and how might you navigate those risks?

Whole-Group Debrief:
- What risks might the parents have perceived in confronting the leadership?
- What are the real risks of being an advocate in an educational system?
- How might you have worked with parents to help them get their needs met?
- What are the real benefits of being an advocate for dismantling inequity, and where might you begin?

Homework: Read "Educational Cultural Negotiators for Students of Color: A Descriptive Study of Racial Advocacy Leaders" by April Warren Grice and Laurence Parker (2018). With your learning partner, design your own debrief questions for facilitating a discussion about the article. The questions should provoke critical thinking. Submit your questions to the lead facilitator. They may be used during Exercise 51.

Exercise 49 Handout: Tips for Becoming a Fearless Equity Warrior

How can you use your privilege, power, or position to empower others? How can you support others through advocacy when they feel like they lack the means or ability to do so? Here are some things to think about as you consider your role as an advocate.

Access the Sting of Injustice

Have you ever felt what it's like to experience injustice or be at the mercy of someone or something that placed you at an unfair disadvantage? Place yourself in the shoes of the affected person, and feel the moral outrage of being at the mercy of a system that you lack the voice or power to challenge. Use that indignation for injustice to fuel your fire to confront an unjust system. Note that if the target has experienced injustices frequently, they may have grown apathetic to the system and simply given in or given up. Understand that it doesn't necessarily mean they don't care. It could mean they feel hopeless, helpless, or overwhelmed or are experiencing racial fatigue.

Choose a Path

Everyone's path to advocacy need not be the same, nor should they be. How you choose to advocate for others is as unique as your personality and skills. Perhaps you choose to voice your opinions in editorials, write scholarly position papers, or petition for better legislation. You may choose to distribute information on social media; campaign for a political candidate who supports social justice; educate parents; or advise administrators, school board members, or politicians. You may choose to teach parents or students how to advocate for themselves. Select a path that is comfortable for you and that uses your unique skill set.

Build a Coalition

Look around. Who else believes what you do? What organizations, networks, or agencies are engaging in the same work? Enlist their support and help. Ask them to join their voices with yours when you speak truth to power. You don't have to stand alone. There are others who will willingly stand with you and elevate an important issue by increasing the volume of voices.

Identify the Decision Makers

Who are the policy leaders and decision makers who can make change happen? Identify them, and craft your message to speak to mutual interests.

One of the tenets of critical race theory is the idea that change happens when there is interest convergence on the part of opposing parties. Therefore, determine who has the power to make a change happen and how the change will serve an interest they hold. Now you're ready to have a conversation!

Confront Bias

Whether it's discipline, teaching, curriculum, or the actions or language of other staff members, recognize and confront bias when you see it. Confrontation does not necessarily equate with hostility. You can challenge something or someone by merely pointing out the inconsistencies with similar practices with other students or staff.

Provide Information, Materials, Opportunities, and Resources

Historically, information, materials, opportunities, and resources have been reserved for the privileged. An advocate throws back the veil of secrecy and extends the same resources to everyone. Be the educator who discusses their own postsecondary academic experiences with students, who helps students make informed decisions about colleges, who provides multiple resources that highlight new ideas, who ventures beyond the classroom to introduce kids to new experiences, who explores various cultures, and who empowers children and parents to lead.

Exercise 50: The Parent Trap

Time: 1–2 months

Materials: Exercise 50 handout

Learning Objective: To design a plan to create a more inclusive, welcoming, and culturally responsive environment for parents

Facilitator Guidelines:

1. Read "The Sewing Bee" scenario to participants. Ask them to form groups of four to five, and pass out the Exercise 50 handout on parent engagement.

2. Complete the handout together.

"The Sewing Bee" Scenario

Caley Elementary School had a large population of Spanish-speaking immigrants. After several years of wringing their hands at the lack of parent involvement at the school, staff members approached parents for suggestions on how they would like to be involved. Much to their surprise, the parents wanted a place where they could sew! Many of the mothers were avid seamstresses who performed contractual work from home. Although their income was small, they began to devote their Tuesday mornings to sewing projects for the school.

Every Tuesday, the parents would set up shop in an empty classroom where they would complete projects, such as sewing quilted backpacks to hang on the back of student chairs. These backpacks provided additional space for students to store books and materials that couldn't fit in their desks. More important, these Tuesday mornings at the school became a time for many parents to socialize, catch up on neighborhood news, become acclimated to the culture of school in their new country, understand the school curriculum, and talk about their families and community issues. What began as a simple parent involvement activity evolved into on-site English as a Second Language classes for parents; on-call translation services; playground and cafeteria monitoring support; and a forum for immigration discussions, activism, and support.

After a year, Caley no longer had a lack of parent involvement. In fact, they were in search of a far larger room for parents to meet. The principal admitted that she never would have thought of a sewing bee as a route to increased parent involvement. Working with parents to design a culturally responsive way in which *they* chose to be involved made all the difference in the world.

Homework: Read "From Family Engagement to Equitable Collaboration" by Ann M. Ishimaru (2019). Design three critical thinking questions for you and your learning partner to discuss when you meet.

Exercise 50 Handout: Looking at Parent Engagement

Directions: How culturally responsive are our parent involvement activities? How do we empower parents to lead? For the next month, we will review the ways we invite parents to be engaged in our school. We will conduct the review in collaboration with parents and respect their voices. By the end of the month, you may have another proverbial sewing bee or something that more closely reflects the cultural values and interests of the community. Begin the process being open to hearing new voices, expanding the range of voices heard, and being flexible on how ideas evolve.

1. List the opportunities parents have to be involved at your school.

2. Mine the data to determine the approximate percentage of parents who are involved in the activities listed (given your student population).

3. If there is a low rate of parent involvement in school activities, determine the data you need to collect to understand why. Ensure you have a plan for how to collect the most accurate and inclusive data from parents (e.g., through focus groups, surveys, suggestion boxes).

4. Disaggregate data and work with parents to devise a plan to increase involvement, given parent input or recommendations.

5. Assess where parents can meet at the school. Is there room for a parent lounge? If so, what would make it welcoming for parents? If not, how can you better accommodate parents so they feel welcome anytime?

Exercise 51: Cultural Negotiating

Time: 30 minutes

Materials: None

Learning Objective: To learn how to be a better advocate

Facilitator Guidelines:

1. Aggregate the best questions submitted by participants in Exercise 49 on the reading "Educational Cultural Negotiators for Students of Color: A Descriptive Study of Racial Advocacy Leaders" by April Warren Grice and Laurence Parker (2018). Prioritize the order in which the questions will be discussed.

2. Facilitate a whole-group discussion of the reading using the questions. Be sure to give credit to the authors of the questions used.

Exercise 52: Welcome to Us

Time: 30 minutes

Materials: Computer and projection screen/space for each team of 10, ballot box, voting slips

Learning Objective: To examine the key messages for new staff coming into an equitable learning community

Facilitator Guidelines:

1. Have participants divide into groups of 10 or fewer. Ask them to storyboard a 10-minute PowerPoint, Prezi, or Keynote onboarding presentation for new staff. The finalized presentations will be showcased in the next meeting.

2. In creating their presentations, participants should

   ▶ Discuss the vision, mission, and culture of the school.

   ▶ Determine key points that new staff members need to know as they enter the school community.

   ▶ Clarify what is crucial for them to know about equity, culture, race, power, and privilege.

   ▶ Advise them of behavioral expectations, particularly in relation to interacting with students.

   ▶ Be creative and innovative. Theirs could be the award-winning selection!

3. After 30 minutes, ask each team to assign the tasks needed to complete the presentation. Have teams select a lead presenter.

Homework: Participants are to complete and refine their 15-minute presentations in preparation for the Onboard Oscars Award Ceremony that will take place during the next session. Presentations can be uploaded to a common internal website for review prior to the next meeting. Voting ballots and a ballot box can be preserved in a common area. Each person receives one voting slip that must be completed in the office. The voting slips may be simple: a sticky note with your preferred selection and one or two reasons why your choice provides the best representation of the school community. You may choose to consider including parents or students in the voting process, especially if students or parents have consented to be videotaped.

Good luck!

Exercise 53: The Onboard Oscars Award Ceremony

Time: 40 minutes

Materials: Computer, projection screen, vote counters, signup sheets for volunteers

Learning Objective: To select an onboarding presentation for new staff that best reflects the ideals of the school community

Facilitator Guidelines:

1. Prior to the meeting, ask a neutral party to tally the votes and provide you with the name of the team that received the most votes.

2. Greet staff in your ballgown or tuxedo, and announce the Onboard Oscar Awards for the most outstanding onboarding presentation for the school.

3. Show the videos for the top two to three submissions.

4. Announce the winner and applaud all the participants!

5. Before you adjourn the meeting, let participants know there are two signup sheets in the room for those who wish to deepen their involvement in the onboarding process:

   ▸ A signup sheet for those who would like to participate in the recruitment, selection, and interviewing of potential new staff.

   ▸ A signup sheet for those who would like to present the onboarding training for new staff.

Exercise 54: To Be or Not to Be

Time: 30 minutes

Materials: None

Learning Objective: To explore what it means to be an ally

Facilitator Guidelines:

1. Have participants divide into groups of four.

2. Explain that each group will discuss six topics; participants will have approximately five minutes to discuss each topic.

Small-Group Discussion:

- Topic 1: List your five closest friends, and discuss them with a partner. Why do you consider these people your closest friends?

- Topic 2: Categorize the five friends by racial category. If one of them has a racial identity different from yours, discuss how their racial experiences influence your relationship. If none of them has a racial identity different from yours, discuss how you interact in a country that is racially diverse without making close friends with someone who is racially diverse. How does that happen, and why?

- Topic 3: If you have friends who are from a historically marginalized racial group, how are you working to end the oppression they are likely experiencing? How have you intentionally tried to understand the oppression they have experienced in the past? For people who are members of historically marginalized racial groups, how have your close friends worked to end the oppression that you are or have experienced? How have they tried to understand it?

- Topic 4: How have you worked to end the oppression of historically marginalized students? (They need not be your own students.) How have you tried to understand their experiences?

- Topic 5: An ally is someone who works to end the oppression of historically marginalized people. Can you have a close friend, colleague, or student from a historically marginalized group who is experiencing racism and oppression and *not* be their ally?

- Topic 6: Are you an ally? What do you potentially risk by being one? What informed your decision to be—or not to be—an ally?

Key Takeaways:

- Having a friend or knowing students from a historically marginalized group does not make you their ally.

- Allies take action. Allies take risks.

Exercise 55: The Bailey Family

Time: 30 minutes

Materials: Exercise 55 handouts 1 and 2

Learning Objective: To explore how inequities can affect everyone in society

Facilitator Guidelines:

1. Have participants read "The Bailey Family" scenario in Exercise 55 handout 1 in small groups and then respond to the small-group discussion questions.

2. Have participants read the "Analogy Reveal" in Exercise 55 handout 2 and then respond to the small-group debrief questions.

Small-Group Discussion:

- How is Junior able to maintain his position of privilege?
- What does Junior fear might happen if any of his siblings comes into power?
- Junior, who flourishes in college, seems to be on the fast-track to success, whereas his siblings struggle at home and in school. How would you explain this situation to Mr. and Mrs. Bailey, who just assume that Junior is more gifted and capable than the other children?

Whole-Group Discussion:

- How long can this situation be sustained?
- What needs to happen?

Small-Group Debrief:

- What are some ways society might try to maintain a position of white supremacy?
- Some people cannot understand the behavioral, emotional, financial, and mental instabilities that others are experiencing in our society. What would you say to them?
- Why is it seemingly so difficult for people to identify with the plight of marginalized or oppressed people? Why would they turn away? Why might they deny the public evidences of oppression and marginalization? How do racism and inequity affect white individuals?

Whole-Group Debrief:

- How long can racism, oppression, or inequity be sustained?
- What needs to happen?

Key Takeaway: It is my best hope that advocacy and leadership were integral to your response to what needs to happen.

Exercise 55 Handout 1: "The Bailey Family" Scenario

Everybody knew the Bailey family. They were the envy of the town—popular, good-looking, athletic, scholarly, and wealthy. They were the family everyone wished they could be. Everyone, that is, except most members of the Bailey family. You see, they had a peculiar way of handling things in their home.

When the Baileys established their home, they made the decision that the oldest child would receive special benefits and privileges that would not be extended to the other children in the family. And so it was. They became parents to the four most extraordinary children in the world: Junior, 18, was a freshman in college; Lillie, 16, and Adam, 14, attended the high school; and Tina, 12, was a middle school student. Each child had exquisite gifts and talents, although those of the three younger siblings went largely ignored because, from the very start, Junior was put in charge of the household.

Junior drove an admirable brand-new sports car. (He got a new one every year). But he wouldn't allow Lillie to have anything more than a 1955 vehicle that broke down every week. Adam was warned that he would never receive a car, and Tina was destined to walk until she could afford better.

Junior also decided the sleeping arrangements. He took the master bedroom and the fourth bedroom for his own TV room. He gave the largest of the remaining bedrooms to his parents, allowed Lillie and Tina to share a room, and allocated Adam to sleep in the unfinished basement. Junior had no chores, of course, but the other children did. Adam washed Junior's car and his parents' cars. Lillie dusted and took out the trash. But poor Tina washed and ironed all the clothes, vacuumed and mopped the floors, shopped and cooked dinner, and cleaned all the bathrooms.

Junior had complete decision-making authority over food rations, clothes selections, discipline decisions, and the purchase of educational materials and toys. At his discretion, the other siblings might get very little to eat or nothing at all; they might receive new shoes or sandals or be relegated to hand-me-downs. They might get toys or a birthday party—if he was so willing.

Occasionally Junior would strike the children if they failed to complete their chores to his satisfaction. He was also known to scold, scream, or call them names if they did not comply with his wishes immediately. The parents listened to the complaints and accusations of the younger siblings, but, in general, they supported Junior in continuing to conduct himself however he chose. They assured the children they were neutral and objective parties.

As you can imagine, this created a tenuous climate in the home. Junior, drunk with power, joined the Association of Sibling Haters, where he learned more insidious ways to torment his siblings and taunt them with symbols of hatred. Meanwhile, the siblings were growing worse for the wear. Lillie started carrying a weapon for protection and began attacking her classmates in school. Adam and Lillie frequently fought. Adam began stealing food and clothes from Junior's stash. Although grappling with bouts of depression, Tina somehow excelled in mathematics, which only infuriated Junior. Her success was an irksome reminder that his position was predicated on his ability to sustain a position of superiority in all things. So he taunted Tina and told her that she would never aspire to anything more than an unplanned pregnancy.

Exercise 55 Handout 2: Analogy Reveal

The United States rose to a position of power after being colonized by British immigrants. They were the envy of the world: popular, good-looking, athletic, scholarly, and wealthy. They were the country everyone wished they could be. Everyone, that is, except growing members of the citizenry. You see, they had a peculiar way of handling things at home.

White males and their offspring received special benefits and privileges that would not be extended to the indigenous population, immigrants, and enslaved peoples. And so it was. They became guardians to the most extraordinary talent in the world. Each citizen had exquisite gifts and talents, although these went largely ignored because, from the very start, only certain people were given a position of leadership and recognition.

Only certain people were granted the opportunity for wealth or freedom or to pursue happiness. Only certain citizens could choose their housing and their careers. Others were made to work long hours for little pay and had limited choices. At the discretion of certain citizens, others got very little to eat or nothing at all; they might receive new shoes or sandals or be relegated to hand-me-downs.

And occasionally, certain citizens would strike others with impunity. They were known to scold, scream, or call other people names if those people did not comply with their wishes. They would burn them, hang them from trees, or shoot them point blank, even when they carried little more than a cell phone for protection. The legal system listened to the complaints and accusations against the ruling citizenry, but it generally supported them in continuing to conduct society however they chose. The legal system assured others that they were neutral and objective parties, even when it was glaringly apparent that they were not.

As you can imagine, this created a tenuous climate in the country. The ruling class formed organizations where they learned more insidious ways to torment their peers and taunt them with symbols of hatred. Meanwhile, things were growing worse for the wear. Random shootings and massacres increased daily. More people started carrying a weapon, and attacks on the general public increased. People banded together to form groups of influence and protection, but they frequently fought among themselves. Accounts of fraud and theft at all levels of society increased, with each person justifying the need to steal from the other. After all, the ruling class was known to hoard food and clothes while limiting others to minimal servings of gruel.

Loneliness and depression increased significantly, even at the youngest levels of society. However, when the marginalized peers somehow excelled despite the odds, it only infuriated some members of the ruling class. After all, if their peers were proficient academically, how could the ruling class continue to maintain its power? The growth and success of their peers were irksome reminders that the position of the ruling class was predicated on its ability to sustain a position of superiority in all things. So the ruling class tried to limit the ability of certain populations to grow and flourish.

Exercise 56: Envisioning the Past

Time: 25 minutes

Materials: Large sticky notes and markers

Learning Objective: To reflect on our growth in cultural competency as a learning community

Facilitator Guidelines:

1. Divide into groups of four to five. Provide a large sticky note sheet for each group, and ask participants to divide the paper into four sections.

2. Explain, "Our school looks and feels different than it did a year ago. Let's critique what we did to get here."

3. Place one question in each of the four sections of the paper:

   ▸ Question 1. Difference: How does our school today compare with where we were a year ago?

   ▸ Question 2. Challenges: What were some issues or challenges we faced during our journey to become more culturally competent?

   ▸ Question 3. Strategies: How did we successfully overcome our challenges and issues?

   ▸ Question 4. Advice: What advice would we give other colleagues about navigating this journey?

4. Groups will discuss each question and record their answers. They have 20 minutes before they report to the whole group.

Whole-Group Debrief:

- What surprised or excited you?

- Which of the strategies that we identified as crucial to overcoming our challenges do we need to employ more often? How can we institutionalize them?

- What advice that we gave to colleagues could we better follow ourselves? How can we institutionalize these practices?

As Quarter 4 Draws to a Close . . .

You deserve a pat on the back and so do your colleagues. Grab the next three people you see, pat them on the back, and let them know how pleased you are to have completed this journey with them. You have made great strides this quarter in your development as a leader in one of the most difficult challenges of our time. This quarter you worked collaboratively with parents to design a better system inclusive of their voice, their culture, and their values. You developed critical thinking questions to help your partner or colleagues discuss issues of race and privilege. You discussed ways to be a better advocate for others and practiced how to do so. It's time to check in and see how you are progressing on this last set of behaviors, skills, and dispositions. Review the "Advocate and Lead" section of the Cultural Competency Continuum (see Figure 7.1). Check any statements with which you agree. Once again, notice and celebrate your progress. The activities in this chapter have prepared you for honing your skills as an equity advocate and leader. Continue to open yourself up to new leadership opportunities. There's no turning back now, you badass educator, you.

Figure 7.1 **Advocate and Lead**

Culturally competent professionals have participatory, collaborative partnerships with stakeholders and are fervent advocates for equitable access and opportunities for all.
STEP 4. ADVOCATE AND LEAD _____I reach out to parents and the community regularly and engage diverse stakeholders in the decision-making process for anything that affects them or the students. _____I empower all stakeholders and encourage open dialogue and dissent. _____I identify barriers that prevent certain populations from full access to services and have taught colleagues ways to remove them. _____I confront racism when I see it. _____I advocate for cultural competency and social justice effectively and professionally. _____I reject any privileges that come with white racial identity and actively work to ensure everyone has equal access and opportunities _____I am a brave equity warrior. (And I've got the scars to prove it.)

8

The Long Road Ahead

If you were charged with deciding what students need to know or be able to do to make the United States a truly great country, would you reinstitute skills and knowledge from a previous era? Would you teach children to segregate themselves physically and socially by race? Would you diminish the intellect and opportunities of women, ignore factors that pollute our environment, and disrespect nonwestern cultures? Would you reinstitute rigorous typewriting courses, girls' sewing classes, and the infamous middle school ballroom dance classes? Would you break out the slide rulers and abacuses to teach math or the Dick and Jane basal readers to teach reading?

God, I hope not. What made America so outstanding is not our ability to repeat the past but to invent the future. What students need to know and be able to do is navigate a global economy. They need the skills to fluidly move between cultures and among people of different hues, languages, and customs and craft an inclusive culture that all are invited to participate in. It would not be wise to use obsolete tools on a future that is being redesigned and under construction as we speak.

Toward that end, we need educators who can bridge the gulf between the past and the future—culturally competent staff who can help students envision a future that is inclusive and equitable and who can advocate alongside them to create it. You now have the foundation. The rest is up to you. I urge you to continue on your journey of cultural competency into the unforeseeable future.

Of course, it's painfully clear that it's going to take more than 20 minutes, 20 hours, or even 20 years to completely shed the racist ideology and rhetoric that have infiltrated our beliefs and values, hypnotized our thinking, robotized our responses, and obscured our vision. But there's no turning back because now you know that many of the narratives you were told about the great American dream were never true of all Americans. If you were hoodwinked into believing the myths of meritocracy, you can free yourself of that narrative. The chances for fair access and opportunity are exponentially more likely if you are a member of a dominant group that disproportionately benefits from privileges that others are denied.

What will make America the outstanding country it can still become is not the continued oppression of people or the hoarding of resources and opportunities. America will be greater when we embrace the ideology of inclusion in our schools and educational institutions and help students create a world in which equity is the norm, rather than a dream.

We've had 60 years of dreaming. Wake up, and let's get this done. We can create an equitable system of opportunity and inclusion for our students by examining things that are under our control: our classrooms, our pedagogy, our behavioral responses, our curricular selections, our policies, our practices, our disciplinary approaches, our interactions, our support, our recommendations, our encouragements, our leadership, our advocacy, and ourselves. You may have little control over institutions and systems outside of your own, but if you shift the atmosphere within your school, that action can potentially have a profound effect on an entire educational ecosystem. To be clear, this is the end goal—to use the knowledge, skills, and dispositions of cultural competency to positively change the trajectory of children's lives.

What You Can Do

I'd like to leave you with some closing thoughts on how you can help create an equitable system of opportunity and inclusion for all our students.

Find Your Voice and Use It

Be kind, assertive, and immediate in challenging colleagues who exhibit racial or ethnic prejudices and biases. If you hear a colleague express a sentiment that is unfair or detrimental to someone's well-being, immediately challenge it with a clarifying question. For example, you might ask

- "What makes you say that?"
- "Why do you think that?"
- "What do you mean by that?"
- "What is the basis for your assumption?"
- "How does that align with our vision for our school?"
- "Can you help me understand . . . ?"

A question can often confront someone without threat while providing an opportunity for the respondent to pause, reflect on their words, or clarify their intention. It's a delicate balance, but we *can* find language that is both kind and advocating by reminding ourselves of the commonalities we share with one another, our students, and our families. Our humanity is a unifying force. If someone's actions or words call into question the dignity or respect that everyone deserves as a member of humanity, find your voice and use it.

Get Connected

Connect with colleagues, organizations, associations, and networks that share like-minded goals in dismantling inequitable systems. Meet others who are active in this work. There are also cultural and educational organizations that have similar goals of creating equitable institutions within your community; by joining with them, you become part of a growing movement. Find others who are striving to create a more equitable educational experience for children; see what they are doing and how you might work together.

Partner with parents who are interested in furthering the goals of social justice within educational systems. Parents and community members are often placed in a hierarchical relationship in which they are expected to adhere to traditional patterns of involvement that are dictated or designed by school officials. By empowering parents to work in collaboration with staff as equal partners in developing policies and procedures that benefit students, schools can dismantle archaic, paternalistic relationships that have limited parents' voice and caged their involvement. Allow parents to design the ways they would like to be involved. Give them equal voice in school improvement efforts. Improving schools works best when it is done *with* parents rather than *to* them. Invite them to professional development trainings and create onsite trainings for parents in cultural competence, antiracism, and equity. I can't emphasize this enough. Empower, rather than police parents. (They are policed enough.)

At a school in Colorado, parents shared with me their experience conducting walk-throughs. Parents were provided a clipboard with a checklist of criteria they deemed important (kindness toward students, fair disciplinary measures, clean classrooms, equitable treatment of students, etc.). The items in question were no surprise to staff because they had been shared with them ahead of time.

Both parents and community members visited the classrooms throughout the morning, looking for evidence of their criteria. During lunch, they discussed their observations with one another. After lunch, they met with the leadership to debrief. The rest of the afternoon was spent preparing their presentation to staff, which took place immediately after dismissal. Not surprisingly, the staff looked forward to the feedback because, most often, it was glowing and complimentary. This practice helped build trust between staff and parents, while empowering parents to have a voice in school policies and procedures that affected their children and that mattered to them. Connect with your parents and community population, and empower them to lead and learn with you. And in return, you will be amazed at what you can accomplish together. Remember, there are pockets of populations that have seldom if ever experienced the fullness of inclusion. Give it to them. It is well overdue.

Elevate Student Voice

As you consider how to empower parents and other stakeholders in creating a more equitable and inclusive school community, don't neglect one of the most significant stakeholders—the students. Students are keenly aware of how decisions made by teachers and school officials affect them. Historically, their voices have been ignored or dismissed in matters of school improvement, social justice, and equity.

Create a brave space where students can discuss their experiences. Guide them in learning how to talk about issues of racism, privilege, and power. Provide leadership courses that include information about their legal rights, how they can protest injustice, and how they can develop as a credible advocate. Seat them at the table when decisions are made about the creation of equitable, fair, and inclusive practices. Explore how other schools are authentically including students in the decision-making and problem-solving process. Students are the focus and the purpose for which we are engaged in this work in schools. Ensure they are integral to the process of improving equitable learning opportunities as well.

Promote Collective Responsibility

Creating a more equitable and inclusive environment involves personal commitment to self-development, but it's also the work of the collective school staff. Dismantling inequity is messy work, which involves tough questions, complex problems, deep emotional ties, confusing feelings, critical thinking, patience building, and time-sensitive work. You have the big picture, but the devil is in the details. Lean on one another to wrestle through them. Celebrate each marker met, each target reached, and each goal accomplished. Remind one another of your ability to accomplish great things together and grow in your collective efficacy to understand and navigate the sociopolitical, economic, and cultural context in which we are tasked to work.

Continue to Ask Yourself the Tough Questions

As you strive to create a more equitable and inclusive environment, continue to confront the tough questions: Who are the folks you are most likely to label? Who do you eye with suspicion and distrust? Who do you help without hesitation? Who do you praise for their efforts and work? Are your actions creating or limiting opportunities for diverse staff and students? If your answers make you uncomfortable, just know that you have more work to do, and that's OK. Just keep moving in the positive direction of understanding your biases and building your cultural competency.

Educate Yourself

Continue to learn and expand your knowledge base on cultural competency and embracing an antiracist identity. Read other books and attend various conferences. Seek out people who look different from you or from members of your family. Intercultural relationships are one of the best ways to help you understand various racial identities and their experiences. It might feel uncomfortable at first, but I encourage you to give it a try.

I was sitting in a coffee shop recently when I noticed an older white woman who kept eyeing me at the next table. She finally asked me about the book I was reading. It was something mildly interesting I was perusing while waiting for a friend. But she found my explanation amusing, and we began to engage in a light conversation. Before she left, she explained she was taking an anti-bias class at her church and her homework assignment had been to have a conversation with someone of a different race or ethnicity. Now I was more than intrigued. "What did you learn?" I asked. She smiled with a hint of embarrassment: "It wasn't as scary as I imagined."

The Beginning

When we began this journey, I was full of hope. And each day my hope is renewed as I visit schools and other organizations that are embracing the idealism of a world in which every person has an equitable opportunity to succeed, where systems that benefit a privileged few are abolished, where schools promote compassion and healing as part of the educational process, where all students are valued, where the multiplicity of culture is accepted, and where someone doesn't have to ask for their life to matter—even if for 400 years it did not.

We, as educators, have the power to change the course of history through our actions every day. We have the privilege of educating and influencing the next president of the United States; the next computer software innovator; or the next Nobel Peace Prize winner, poet laureate, or university president. We never know how far our influence will extend.

You can change the trajectory of our racist history. The negative narratives about racial hierarchy, as well as the systems of privilege and institutions that perpetuate them, can be dismantled through knowledge, action, and advocacy. It may feel unfamiliar, uncomfortable, and even daunting, but once you accept your calling as advocate or ally by virtue of your responsibility as educator, I believe you will also find that it isn't as scary as you may have imagined. There's a long road ahead, but just think! Look how far we have come already!

Acknowledgments

Thanks to Genny Ostertag, Liz Wegner, and the team at ASCD. I can't thank you enough for your feedback and support. Dr. Dorothy Garrison-Wade, my "shero," my friend, my mentor. I am forever grateful for your encouragement and mentorship. Justin and J.R., I've been grinning with pride since I first held you in my arms. Your brilliance and talent leave me in awe. I hope to read your books and see your films someday. I know that day will come. And Steve, my wonderfully "woke" husband and ally, you have been my critical friend and thought partner through every step of this journey. Your insight, intellect, and attention to detail amaze and inspire me everyday. You remain unquestionably the Love. Of. My. Life. Finally, foremost, and above all, my work is a reflection of one indelible truth: To God be the glory. Great things He hath done.

Homework Handouts

You can also access the homework handouts online: www.ascd.org/ASCD/pdf/books/mayfield2020.pdf

Exercise 4 Homework Handout: Culture, Literacy, and Power in Families

Read "Culture, Literacy, and Power in Family–Community–School–Relationships" by Concha Delgado Gaitan (2012). Then discuss the following questions with your learning partner.

The Language and Culture of Schooling

- According to the author, why are some parents excluded from participating in their child's schooling?
- What is the relationship among language, culture, and power in schools?
- How do immigrant parents learn about the language of schooling in your school? How might you support this effort?
- How does your school buffer the distress of dislocation for immigrant families? How might you support this effort?
- How does your knowledge of a student's home culture influence their schooling?

Culturally Responsive Parent–School–Community Connections

- What powers are shared between parents and educators in your school? In your classroom? What more can you do?
- What are some of the collective values of families in your school community? How did you determine them?
- What is the common culture shared between families and the school? In what ways does the school culture allow all to participate and express themselves in meaningful ways? What more can you do?

Empowerment

- What does collective parent engagement look like in your school? What is your role in supporting it?
- Why would an educator need to empower parents who historically have been marginalized? How does that benefit the schooling of all children?

Exercise 10 Homework Handout:
Rethinking Bilingual Instruction

Read "Rethinking Bilingual Instruction" by Patricia Gándara (2015). Then discuss the following questions with your learning partner.

Cognitive Advantages: The Evidence Grows
- Discuss the advantages of bilingualism.

Labor Market Advantages: The Picture Becomes Clearer
- What connections can you make between racial/ethnic identity and the valuation of bilingual skills in our culture?
- When bilingual skills are negated in schools, who has the power and who does not?
- What does language development look like when both monolingual and bilingual stakeholders share power?

How Schools Can Foster Bilingualism
- What do you do to support students who are bilingual? What can you do?
- What do you do to support students who wish to be bilingual? How do you determine if they or their parents have this interest?

Exercise 11 Homework Handout: Another Inconvenient Truth

Read "Another Inconvenient Truth: Race and Ethnicity Matter" by Willis D. Hawley and Sonja Nieto (2010). Then discuss the following questions with your learning partner.

- Describe your personal identity—how you see yourself and the unique characteristics or traits that you embody.

- Is the way you look part of your identity? What do the authors state is wrong with being colorblind toward your students?

- What other nonproductive beliefs of educators do the authors debunk?

- Reread the list of recommended race and ethnicity teaching practices in the article. Which ones, if any, would *not* be beneficial for all students? Which ones are you currently using? Which ones require more professional development, knowledge, and support to implement? What next steps can you take to acquire the necessary training, if needed?

- What insights did you gain from this article? What strategies are you prepared to try tomorrow?

Exercise 16 Homework Handout: Embodying Decoloniality

Read "Embodying Decoloniality: Indigenizing Curriculum and Peda-gogy" by Karlee D. Fellner (2018). Then discuss the following questions with your learning partner.

- What might be an example of colonial ideology (i.e., the way colonial immigrants thought about indigenous people, Mexican people, or Black people, as well as their land and their rights)?

- How were indigenous people blamed for the violence perpetrated on them? What purpose did it serve? How were other people of color blamed for the violence perpetrated on them? What purpose did it serve?

- The author recommends addressing the ways colonization has affected relationships in the community as an opportunity to challenge unhealthy internalized patterns. How has colonial ideology affected relationships in communities of color?

- Fellner recommends discussing internalized oppression with "survivance and compassion." With your partner, model a five-minute discussion on internalized oppression and racism with compassion for the generational survivors of violent acts and ongoing marginalization.

Exercise 17 Homework Handout: The Stereotype Within

Read "The Stereotype Within" by Marc Elrich (2002). Then discuss the following questions with your learning partner.

1. Where do you believe the students learned the negative stereotypes about Black people?
2. Which stereotypes have you heard and where did you hear them?
3. Do you believe this phenomenon is still relevant and occurring with students today? Why or why not?

Action Research Project: Find out how much has changed in the past 20 years. Give each student in your class two sheets of paper. Tell the students you are conducting research that will help you to be a better teacher. All the responses will be kept confidential. On one sheet, ask them to write down everything they know to be true about white people. On the other sheet, ask them to write down everything they know to be true about Black people. Collect the responses and read them alone. What do you see? Discuss with your partner next week.

**Exercise 18 Homework Handout:
Teachers, Please Learn Our Names**

Read "Teachers, Please Learn Our Names! Racial Microaggressions and the K–12 Classroom" by Rita Kohli and Daniel G. Solórzano (2012). Then discuss the following questions with your learning partner.

History of Racism in Schools

- Do you correct someone if they mispronounce your name? Why or why not?
- When does it become racist to mispronounce someone's name?
- The authors state on page 446 that "it is important to understand racism beyond blatant and overt acts of discrimination." What other forms can it take?
- When would encouraging a student to change their name to an American pronunciation be racist?

Critical Race Theory

- Discuss the five tenets of critical race theory. (These are listed in the article.) Describe them in your own words to your partner. (You will see evidence of these tenets in many of our research readings, so it is good to familiarize yourself with them.)

Racial Microaggressions

- What is a racial microaggression, and how could mispronouncing a name be considered one?
- Discuss the last time you felt slighted. What happened, and how did it make you feel?

Internalized Racism

- Underline the definition of internalized racism provided in the article. What are the potential long-term effects when a person of color internalizes racism? How might this affect their schooling experiences?

Racial Microaggressions and Names in School

- Discuss the examples of racial microaggressions and student names in schools. Which one resonated with you, and why?

Internalized Racial Microaggression

- Discuss the examples of internalized racial microaggressions. Which one resonated with you, and why?

Addressing Racial Microaggressions and Internalized Racial Microaggressions in School

- Discuss the three recommendations provided in the article. What can you do differently to ensure your students don't experience microaggressions or internalize racism as a result of your influence?

**Exercise 19 Homework Handout:
Unpacking Internalized Racism**

Read "Unpacking Internalized Racism: Teachers of Color Striving for Racially Just Classrooms" by Rita Kohli (2014). Then discuss the following questions with your learning partner.

- Analyze the teachers' remarks to Ashley. Why might they have been detrimental to her as she developed her self-identity? How might they have contributed to her internalizing racism (i.e., accepting a racial hierarchy and negative deficit ideology about people of color)? When have you made or heard someone else make a similar remark about a person of color?

- Examine the subtle ways the author notes that white supremacy is reinforced in schools (see p. 371 of the article), and consider your own school. What messages do you give your students about language? Do those messages promote a preference for one language over another? What messages do you give your students about curriculum? Do those messages promote one culture over another?

- Why might it be important for teachers of color to build cultural competency?

- How would you recognize a person of color who had internalized racism?

- What can you do to prevent students from internalizing racism?

Exercise 20 Homework Handout: They Don't Know Anything!

Read "'They Don't Know Anything!' Latinx Immigrant Children Appropriating the Oppressor's Voice" by Lilia D. Monzó (2016). Then discuss the following questions with your learning partner.

- What is the relationship between identity development and internalized racism?

- How might violence in communities be related to internalized racism?

- Do you agree or disagree with the author's claim that the education system is complicit in preserving inter-ethnic conflict through policy and practice? Support your position with specific policy or practice examples from your school or district.

- What kinds of policies or practices might one find in an educational institution where the community of color is viewed through a deficit lens (i.e., that something is wrong with them that needs to be fixed)? For example, this might include rigid disciplinary policies that require students to be escorted in lines throughout the institution.

- What are the implications for educators who desire to help parents navigate school contexts more effectively?

Exercise 25 Homework Handout: The Power of Culture

After reading the article "'The Fish Becomes Aware of the Water in Which It Swims': Revealing the Power of Culture in Shaping Teaching Identity" by Yuli Rahmawati and Peter C. Taylor (2018), complete the questions below *before* meeting with your learning partner. Once you meet, discuss your reactions to the article and your responses to the questions.

1. Finish the sentence below and include
    ▸ Where you were born.
    ▸ Your parents' cultural norms.
    ▸ Where you were raised.
    ▸ The influence of your parents' culture on your cultural identity.

I'm _____

_____.

2. What different values, beliefs, and practices have you learned as an adult? How have you adapted, if at all, to the current cultural values to which you have been introduced?

_____

_____

_____.

3. How does your cultural background affect your expectations of students? How does it affect your interactions with them?

_____

_____

_____.

4. What ideals did you have about your teaching identity when you entered the field? How, if at all, have they shifted or changed?

_____

_____

_____.

5. How does your cultural identity influence your teaching practice?

_____

_____

_____.

Exercise 27 Homework Handout: More Than a Metaphor

Read "More Than a Metaphor: The Contribution of Exclusionary Discipline to a School-to-Prison Pipeline" by Russell J. Skiba, Mariella I. Arredondo, and Natasha T. Williams (2014). Then discuss the following questions with your learning partner.

- According to the article, how widespread is the use of exclusionary discipline? Is it increasing?
- How widespread is the use of exclusionary discipline at our school? Has it increased since last year? The year before?
- According to the article, who is at risk for exclusionary discipline? Who is at risk for exclusionary discipline at our school?
- How does disciplinary removal affect educational opportunity and school engagement?
- How does school suspension affect dropout rates. Why?
- Review the Discipline Disparities Research-to-Practice Collaborative's recommendations for reducing the use of exclusionary discipline and addressing disciplinary disparities. Which ones, if any, are you currently employing? Which ones might you consider?

Exercise 33 Homework Handout: Becoming a More Culturally Responsive Teacher

Read "Becoming a More Culturally Responsive Teacher by Identifying and Reducing Microaggressions in Classrooms and School Communities" by Jacqueline Darvin (2018). Then discuss the following questions with your learning partner.

- The author gave multiple examples of microaggressions that included more than racial aggressions. What kinds of microaggressions have you experienced?

- Discuss the recommendations from the article on ways to address or reduce microaggressions in schools. Which ones, if any, did you find useful?

- How did this article expand your thinking about microaggressions, pain, or mistreatment by others?

- Why might some children experience more microaggressions than others? What is your plan to reduce the microaggressions you observe?

Exercise 35 Homework Handout: White Fatigue

Read "White Fatigue: Naming the Challenge in Moving from an Individual to a Systemic Understanding of Racism" by Joseph E. Flynn Jr. (2015). Then discuss the following questions with your learning partner.

- What examples have you seen or experienced of the following phenomena, as defined in the article?
  - ► White fatigue
  - ► Racial battle fatigue
  - ► White people fatigue syndrome
  - ► White guilt
  - ► White fragility
- Although the framework for White Racial Identity Development is theoretical, were there any stages with which you could identify personally? If so, which ones?
  - ► Contact
  - ► Disintegration
  - ► Reintegration
  - ► Pseudo-independence
  - ► Immersion–emersion
  - ► Autonomy
- According to the author, how has racism affected white people? What are your thoughts on how racism has affected white people? Can you provide examples of how it has affected you?

Exercise 45 Homework Handout: Everyday Colorism

Read "Everyday Colorism: Reading in the Language Arts Classroom" by Sarah L. Webb (2019). Then discuss the following questions with your learning partner.

- What are the different ways people's appearances and physical features affect their lives? Why might two sisters have different life outcomes if one has light brown skin and the other has dark brown skin?

- Black women often make a distinction between hair textures and deem some women as having "good" hair. Knowing what you do about colorism now, how do you suppose that term is defined? What constitutes "good" hair? Why qualifies it to be "good?" And how might some women characterize hair that was not? What do you think when you see students with hair texture that is drastically unlike yours? How do you characterize it?

- There is a movement among people of color to wear their hair the way it grows out of their head—natural. What restrictions, biases, or prejudices, if any, does the school impose on girls who choose to do so? Why?

- In some cultures, there was a "paper bag" rule. Anyone darker than the paper bag was denied access, privileges, or jobs that people lighter than the paper bag could acquire. How might rules such as this or other ways distinctions were made between the color of a person within the same race cause divisions in families, friendships, and relationships?

- Colorism happens in every racial and ethnic category. Why would it be important to discuss colorism with students? How can you mitigate its effects among your students? How would you discuss colorism with your students? What texts or resources would you use?

- Look at the resources, pictures, and messages around your school. Do they reflect the full range of colors that people represent?

- Consider the students who were referred for disciplinary referrals this month. How many were dark skinned versus lighter skin toned? How might you unmask colorism hidden within educational interactions?

- What equitable approaches are needed to support the positive identity development of students with dark skin or kinky hair? What might they need above and beyond other students of color?

References

Abul, P. (2008). *The struggle for black history: Foundations for a critical black pedagogy in education*. Lanham, MD: University Press of America.

Alexander, M. (2010). *The New Jim Crow: Mass incarceration in the age of colorblindness*. New York: The New Press.

Allen, S. (2008). Eradicating the achievement gap: History, education, and reformation. *Black History Bulletin, 71*(1), 13–17.

Amatea, E. S., Cholewa, B., & Mixon, K. A. (2012). Influencing preservice teachers' attitudes about working with low-income and/or ethnic minority families. *Urban Education, 47*(4), 801–834.

Anderson, J. D. (1980). Philanthropic control over private black higher education. In R. F. Arnove (Ed.), *Philanthropy and cultural imperialism: The foundations at home and abroad* (pp. 147–177). Boston: G. K. Hall.

Anderson, K. L., & Davis, B. M. (2012). *Creating culturally considerate schools: Educating without bias*. Thousand Oaks, California: Corwin.

Andrews, F. E. (2007). The role of educational leaders in implementing a culturally responsive pedagogy designed to increase the learning opportunities for diverse students. *Academic Leadership, 4*(4), 1–10.

Anyon, J. (1997). *Ghetto schooling: A political economy of urban educational reform*. New York: Teachers College Press.

Apple, M. W. (2009). Is racism in education an accident? *Educational Policy, 23*(4), 651–659.

Atkinson, P. (1993). *Brown vs. Topeka: Desegregation and miseducation*. Chicago: African American Images.

Bae, S., Holloway, S., Li, J., & Bempechat, J. (2008). Mexican-American students' perceptions of teachers' expectations: Do perceptions differ depending on student achievement levels? *Urban Review, 40*(2), 210–225.

Banks, J., Cookson, P., Gay, G., Hawley, W. D., Irvine, J. J., Nieto, S., . . . Stephan, W. G. (2001). Diversity within unity: Essential principles for teaching and learning in a multicultural society. *Phi Delta Kappan, 83*(3), 196.

Batson, C. D., Chang, J., Orr, R., & Rowland, J. (2002). Empathy, attitudes, and action: Can feeling for a member of a stigmatized group motivate one to help the group? *Personality and Social Psychology Bulletin, 28*(12).

Berliner, D. C. (2010). Are teachers responsible for low achievement by poor students? *Education Digest, 75*(7), 4–8.

Bilias-Lolis, E., Gelber, N. W., Rispoli, K. M., Bray, M. A., & Maykel, C. (2017). On promoting understanding and equity through compassionate educational practice: Toward a new inclusion. *Psychology in the Schools, 54*(10).

Blackmon, D. A. (2009). *Slavery by another name: The re-enslavement of black Americans from the Civil War to World War II*. New York: Anchor Books.

Blackmore, J. (2009). Leadership for social justice: A transnational dialogue. *Journal of Research on Leadership Education 4*(1), 1–10.

Boyd, B. A., & Correa, V. I. (2005). Developing a framework for reducing the cultural clash between African American parents and the special education system. *Multicultural Perspectives, 7*(2), 3–11.

Buckley, J. B., & Quaye, S. J. (2016). A vision of social justice in intergroup dialogue. *Race, Ethnicity, and Education, 19*(5), 1117–1139.

Burch, A. D. S. (2018, October 26). How "gardening while black" almost landed this Detroit man in jail. *New York Times.* Retrieved from https://www.nytimes.com/2018/10/26/us/white-women-calling-police-black-men.html

Capper, C. A. (2015). The 20th-year anniversary of critical race theory in education: Implications for leading to eliminate racism. *Educational Administration Quarterly, 51*(5), 791–833.

Carruthers, C. K., & Wanamaker, M. H. (2013). Closing the gap? The effect of private philanthropy on the provision of African-American schooling in the U.S. south. *Journal of Public Economics, 101,* 53–67.

Cicetti-Turro, D. (2007). Straight talk: Talking across race in schools. *Multicultural Perspectives, 9*(1), 45–49.

Clark, P., Zygmunt, E., & Howard, T. (2016). Why race and culture matter in schools, and why we need to get this right: A conversation with Dr. Tyrone Howard. *Teacher Educator, 51*(4), 268–276.

Condron, D. J. (2009). Social class, school and non-school environments, and black/white inequalities in children's learning. *American Sociological Review, 74*(5), 683–708.

Cornell, D., & Limber, S. P. (2015). Law and policy on the concept of bullying at school. *American Psychologist, 70*(4), 333–343.

Cross, B. E. (2007). Urban school achievement gap as a metaphor to conceal U.S. apartheid education. *Theory into Practice, 46*(3), 247–255.

Cross, W. E., Jr., Parham, T. A., & Helms, J. E. (1991). The stages of black identity development: Nigrescence models. In R. Jones (Ed.), *Black psychology* (3rd ed.). San Francisco: Cobb and Henry.

Danielson, C. (2007). *Enhancing professional practice: A framework for teaching* (2nd ed.). Alexandria, VA: ASCD.

Darder, A. (2002). *Reinventing Paulo Freire: A pedagogy of love.* Boulder, CO: Westview Press.

Darvin, J. (2018). Becoming a more culturally responsive teacher by identifying and reducing microaggressions in classrooms and school communities. *Journal for Multicultural Education, 12*(1), 2–9.

Day-Vines, N. L., & Day-Hairston, B. O. (2005, February). Culturally congruent strategies for addressing the behavioral needs of urban, African American male adolescents. *Professional School Counseling, 8*(3), 236–243.

Decety, J., Huerta, S., Batson, C. D., Edwards, A., Correll, J., Echols, S. C., . . . Hodges, S. D. (2011). *Empathy: From bench to bedside.* Cambridge, MA: MIT Press.

DeCuir-Gunby, J. T., Taliaferro, J. D., & Greenfield, D. (2010). Educators' perspectives on culturally relevant programs for academic success: The American excellence association. *Education and Urban Society, 42,* 184–204.

DeLuca, C., Bolden, B., & Chan, J. (2017). Systemic professional learning through collaborative inquiry: Examining teachers' perspectives. *Teaching and Teacher Education, 67,* 67–78.

DiAngelo, R. (2011). White fragility. *International Journal of Critical Pedagogy, 3*(3), 54.

DiAngelo, R., & Sensoy, Ö. (2014). Getting slammed: White depictions of race discussions as arenas of violence. *Race Ethnicity and Education, 17*(1), 103–128.

Drescher, M. A., Korsgaard, M. A., Welpe, I. M., Picot, A., & Wigand, R. T. (2014). The dynamics of shared leadership: Building trust and enhancing performance. *Journal of Applied Psychology, 99*(5), 771–783.

Elrich, M. (2002). The stereotype within. *Black History Bulletin*, 01/2002, Volume 65, Issue 1/2.

Epstein, J. L., Galindo, C. L., & Sheldon, S. B. (2011). Levels of leadership: Effects of district and school leaders on the quality of school programs of family and community involvement. *Educational Administration Quarterly, 47*(3), 462–495.

Farinde-Wu, A., Glover, C. P., & Williams, N. N. (2017). It's not hard work; it's heart work: Strategies of effective, award-winning culturally responsive teachers. *Urban Review, 49*(2), 279–299.

Fasching-Varner, K. J. (2009). No! The team ain't alright! The institutional and individual problematics of race. *Social Identities: Journal for the Study of Race, Nation, and Culture, 15*(6), 811–829.

Fellner, K. D. (2018). Embodying decoloniality: Indigenizing curriculum and pedagogy. *American Journal of Community Psychology, 62*(3/4), 283–293.

Fiedler, C. R., Chiang, B., Van Haren, B., Jorgensen, J., Halberg, S., & Boreson, L. (2008). Culturally responsive practices in schools: A checklist to address disproportionality in special education. *Teaching Exceptional Children, 40*(5), 52–59.

Finnigan, K. S., & Stewart, T. J. (2009). Leading change under pressure: An examination of principal leadership in low-performing schools. *Journal of School Leadership, 19*(5), 586–618.

Flynn, J. E. (2015). White fatigue: Naming the challenge in moving from an individual to a systemic understanding of racism. *Multicultural Perspectives, 17*(3), 115–124.

Ford, D. Y., & Moore, J. L. (2013). Understanding and reversing underachievement, low achievement, and achievement gaps among high-ability African American males in urban school contexts. *Urban Review, 45*(4), 399–415.

Freire, P. (2003). From pedagogy of the oppressed. In A. Darder, M. Baltodano, & R. Torres (Eds.), *The critical pedagogy reader*. New York: Routledge Farmer.

Fullan, M. (2005). 8 forces for leaders of change. *Journal of Staff Development, 26*(4), 54–64.

Gaitan, C. D. (2012). Culture, literacy, and power in family–community–school-relationships. *Theory into Practice, 51*(4), 305–311.

Gándara, P. (2015). Rethinking bilingual education. *Educational Leadership, 72* (6), 60–64.

Gay, G. (2002). Dividing the pie more fairly: Improving the achievement of students of color. *Journal of Thought, 37*(4), 51–64.

Gay, G. (2010). *Culturally responsive teaching: Theory, research, and practice.* New York: Teachers College Press.

Gay, G., & Kirkland, K. (2003). Developing cultural critical consciousness and self-reflection in preservice teacher education. *Theory into Practice, 42*(3), 181–187.

Ginsberg, M. B. (2005). Cultural diversity, motivation, and differentiation. *Theory into Practice, 44*, 218–225.

Glazier, J. A. (2003). Moving closer to speaking the unspeakable: White teachers talking about race. *Teacher Education Quarterly, 30*(1), 73–94.

Gregory, A., Skiba, R. J., & Noguera, P. A. (2010). The achievement gap and the discipline gap: Two sides of the same coin. *Educational Researcher, 39*(1), 59–68.

Grice, W. A., & Parker, L. (2018). Educational cultural negotiators for students of color: A descriptive study of racial advocacy leaders. *Race Ethnicity and Education, 21*(1), 45-62

Griner, A. C., & Stewart, M. L. (2013). Addressing the achievement gap and disproportionality through the use of culturally responsive teaching practices. *Urban Education, 48*(4), 585–621.

Hart, P. S. E. (2002). Race, ethnicity, and public education. *Trotter Review 14*(1).

Hartman, R. J., Johnston, E., & Hill, M. (2017). Empathetic design: A sustainable approach to school change. *Discourse and Communication for Sustainable Education, 8*(2), 38–56.

Hawley, W. D., & Nieto, S. (2010). Another inconvenient truth: Race and ethnicity matter. *Educational Leadership, 68*(3), 66–71.

Haycock, K. (2006). No more invisible kids. *Educational Leadership, 64*(3), 38–42.

Heifetz, R. A. (1994). *Leadership without easy answers*. Cambridge, MA: Belknap Press of Harvard University Press.

Helms, J. E. (1990). *Black and white racial identity: Theory, research and practice*. Westport, CT: Greenwood Press.

Helms, J. E. (1992). *A race is a nice thing to have: A guide to being a white person or understanding the white persons in your life*. Topeka, KS: Content Communications.

Helms, J. E. (1995). An update of Helm's white and people of color racial identity models. In J. G. Ponterotto, J. M. Casas, L. A. Suzuki, & C. M. Alexander (Eds.), *Handbook of multicultural counseling* (pp. 181–198). Thousand Oaks, CA: Sage.

Helms, J. E., & Cook, D. A. (1999). *Using race and culture in counseling and psychotherapy: Theory and process*. Boston: Allyn & Bacon.

Helms, J. E., Nicolas, G., & Green, C. E. (2012). Racism and ethnoviolence as trauma: Enhancing professional and research training. *Traumatology: An International Journal, 18*(1), 65–74.

Howard, T. C. (2010). *Why race and culture still matter: Closing the achievement gap in America's classrooms*. New York: Teachers College Press.

Howard, T. C., & Navarro, O. (2016). Critical race theory 20 years later: Where do we go from here? *Urban Education, 51*, 253–273.

Howley, A., Woodrum, A., Burgess, L., & Rhodes, M. (2009). Planning for culturally responsive leadership: Insights from a study of principals of exemplary schools. *Educational Planning, 18*(3), 12–26.

Ishimaru, A. M. (2019). From family engagement to equitable collaboration. *Educational Policy, 33*(2), 350–385.

Jay, M. (2009). Race-ing through the school day: African American educators' experiences with race and racism in schools. *International Journal of Qualitative Studies in Education, 22*(6), 671–685.

Johannesen, R. L., Valde, K. S., & Whedbee, K. E. (2013). *Ethics in Communication* (6th ed.). Long Grove, IL: Waveland Press.

Kieran, L., & Anderson, C. (2018). Connecting Universal Design for Learning with culturally responsive teaching. *Education and Urban Society*.

King, W. (2005). *African American childhoods: Historical perspectives from slavery to civil rights*. New York: Palgrave Macmillan.

Kohli, R. (2014). Unpacking internalized racism: Teachers of color striving for racially just classrooms. *Race Ethnicity and Education, 17*(3), 367–387.

Kohli, R., & Solórzano, D. G. (2012). Teachers, please learn our names! Racial microaggressions and the K–12 classroom. *Race Ethnicity and Education, 15*(4), 441–462.

Ladson-Billings, G. (1995). But that's just good teaching. The case for culturally responsive pedagogy. *Theory into Practice, 34*(3), 159–165.

Lerone, B. (1975). *The shaping of black America*. Chicago: Johnson Publishing.

Linder, C. (2015). Navigating guilt, shame, and fear of appearing racist: A conceptual model of antiracist white feminist identity development. *Journal of College Student Development, 56*(6), 535–550.

Lindsey, R. B., Roberts, L. M., & CampbellJones, F. (2005). *The culturally proficient school: An implementation guide for school leaders*. Thousand Oaks, CA: Corwin.

Lindsey, R. B., Robins, K. N., & Terrell, R. D. (2003). *Cultural proficiency: A manual for school leaders* (2nd ed.). Thousand Oaks, CA: Corwin.

Martin, D. (2014). Good education for all? Student race and identity development in the multicultural classroom. *International Journal of Intercultural Relations, 39*(0), 110–123.

Marzano, R. J. (2007). *The art and science of teaching: A comprehensive framework for effective instruction.* Alexandria, VA: ASCD.

Marzano, R. J., Pickering, D. J., & Pollock, J. E. (2001). *Classroom instruction that works: Research-based strategies for increasing student achievement.* Alexandria, VA: ASCD.

Marzano, R. J., Waters, T., & McNulty, B. A. (2005). *School leadership that works: From research to results.* Alexandria, VA: ASCD; Aurora, CO: McREL.

McGuinn, P. (2012). Stimulating reform: Race to the Top, competitive grants, and the Obama education agenda. *Educational Policy, 26*(1), 136–159.

McIntosh, P. (1989, July/August). White privilege: Unpacking the invisible backpack. *Peace and Freedom.*

Mezirow, J. (2003). Transformative learning as discourse. *Journal of Transformative Education, 1*(1), 58–63.

Middleton, V. A. (2002). Increasing pre-service teachers' diversity beliefs and commitment. *Urban Review, 34*(4), 343–361.

Milner, H. R. (2010). *Start where you are, but don't stay there: Understanding diversity, opportunity gaps, and teaching in today's classrooms.* Cambridge, MA: Harvard Education Press.

Monroe, C. (2005). Understanding the discipline gap through the cultural lens: Implications for African American students. *Intercultural Education, 16*(4), 317–330.

Monzó, L. D. (2016). "They don't know anything!": Latinx immigrant students appropriating the oppressor's voice. *Anthropology & Education Quarterly, 47*(2), 148–166.

National Center for Education Statistics. (2019a). The condition of education. Public high school graduation rates. Figure 2: Adjusted cohort graduation rate (ACGR) for public high school students, by race/ethnicity: 2016–17. Retrieved from https://nces.ed.gov/programs/coe/indicator_coi.asp

National Center for Education Statistics. (2019b). Status and trends in the education of racial and ethnic groups. Indicator 4: Children living in poverty. Figure 4.1: Percentage of children under age 18 in families living in poverty based on the official poverty measure, by race/ethnicity: 2000 through 2016. Retrieved from https://nces.ed.gov/programs/raceindicators/indicator_rad.asp#1

National Center for Education Statistics. (2019c). Status and trends in the education of racial and ethnic groups. Indicator 10: Reading achievement. Figure 10.1. Average National Assessment of Educational Progress (NAEP) reading scale scores of 4th-grade students, by race/ethnicity: Selected years, 1992–2017. Retrieved from https://nces.ed.gov/programs/raceindicators/indicator_rca.asp#1

National Center for Education Statistics. (2019d). Status and trends in the education of racial and ethnic groups. Indicator 15: Retention, suspension, expulsion. Figure 15.1: Percentage of elementary and secondary school students retained in grade, by race/ethnicity: 2000–2016. Retrieved from https://nces.ed.gov/programs/raceindicators/indicator_rda.asp#1

National Center for Education Statistics. (2019e). Status and trends in the education of racial and ethnic groups. Indicator 15: Retention, suspension, expulsion. Figure 15.3: Percentage of public school students who received out-of-school suspensions, by race/ethnicity and sex: 2013–14. Retrieved from https://nces.ed.gov/programs/raceindicators/indicator_rda.asp#3

National Center for Education Statistics. (2019f). Status and trends in the education of racial and ethnic groups. Spotlight A: Characteristics of public school teachers by race/ethnicity. Figure A.1: Percentage distribution of teachers in public elementary and secondary schools, by race/ethnicity: School years 2003–04 and 2015–16. Retrieved from https://nces.ed.gov/programs/raceindicators/spotlight_a.asp#1

Nelson, T. H., Deuel, A., Slavit, D., & Kennedy, A. (2010). Leading deep conversations in collaborative inquiry groups. *The Clearing House, 83*(5), 175–179.

Olafsen, A. H., Deci, E. L., & Halvari, H. (2018). Basic psychological needs and work motivation: A longitudinal test of directionality. *Motivation and Emotion, 42*(2), 178–189.

Orfield, G., & Eaton, S. (1996). *Dismantling desegregation: The quiet reversal of Brown v. Board of Education.* New York: The New Press.

Parsons, A. A., Walsemann, K. M., Jones, S. J., Knopf, H., & Blake, C. E. (2018). Parental involvement: Rhetoric of inclusion in an environment of exclusion. *Journal of Contemporary Ethnography, 47*(1), 113–139.

Parsons, S. C., & Brown, P. U. (2001). Educating for diversity: An invitation to empathy and action. *Action in Teacher Education, 23*(3), 1–4.

Patterson, K., Grenny, J., McMillan, R., & Switzler, A. (2012). *Crucial conversations: Tools for talking when the stakes are high.* New York: McGraw Hill.

Piazza, S. V., Rao, S., & Protacio, M. S. (2015). Converging recommendations for culturally responsive literacy practices: Students with learning disabilities, English language learners, and socioculturally diverse learners. *International Journal of Multicultural Education, 17*(3), 1–20.

Pierce, C. (1970). Offensive mechanisms. In F. Barbour (Ed.), *In the black seventies.* Boston: Porter Sargent.

Pierce, C., Carew, J., Pierce-Gonzalez, D., & Willis, D. (1978). An experiment in racism: TV commercials. In C. Pierce (Ed.), *Television and education.* Beverly Hills, CA: Sage.

Raffel, J. (1980). *The politics of school desegregation.* Philadelphia: Temple University Press.

Rahmawati, Y., & Taylor, P. C. (2018). "The fish becomes aware of the water in which it swims": Revealing the power of culture in shaping teaching identity. *Cultural Studies of Science Education, 13*(2), 525–537.

Rivera-McCutchen, R. L. (2014). The moral imperative of social justice leadership: A critical component of effective practice. *Urban Review, 46*(4), 747–763.

Sampson, D., & Garrison-Wade, D. (2011). Cultural vibrancy: Exploring the preferences of African American children toward culturally relevant and non-culturally relevant lessons. *The Urban Review, 43*(2), 279–309.

Scribner, J. D., & Reyes, P. (1999). Creating learning communities for high-performing Hispanic students: A conceptual framework. In P. Reyes, J. D. Scribner, & A. P. Scribner (Eds.), *Lessons from high performing Hispanic schools* (pp. 188–210). New York: Teachers College Press.

Sergiovanni, T. J. (2004). Collaborative cultures and communities of practice. *Principal Leadership: High School Edition, 5*(1), 48–52.

Simoes, P. M. M., & Esposito, M. (2014). Improving change management: How communication nature influences resistance to change. *Journal of Management Development, 33*(4), 324–341.

Skiba, R. J., Arredondo, M. I., & Williams, N. T. (2014). More than a metaphor: The contribution of exclusionary discipline to a school-to-prison pipeline. *Equity & Excellence in Education, 47*(4), 546–564.

Smith, L., Kashubeck-West, S., Payton, G., & Adams, E. (2017). White professors teaching about racism: Challenges and rewards. *The Counseling Psychologist, 45*(5), 651–668.

Steele, C. (2010). *Whistling Vivaldi: How stereotypes affect us and what we can do.* New York: W.W. Norton.

Sue, D. W. (2004). Whiteness and ethnocentric monoculturalism: Making the "invisible" visible. *American Psychologist, 59*(8), 761–769.

Sue, D. W. (2010). *Microaggressions in everyday life: Race, gender, and sexual orientation.* Hoboken, NJ: Wiley.

Sue, D. W. (2015). *Race talk and the conspiracy of silence: Understanding and facilitating difficult dialogues on race.* Hoboken, NJ: Wiley.

Taliaferro, J., & DeCuir-Gunby, J. (2008). African American educators' perspectives on the advanced placement opportunity gap. *Urban Review, 40*(2), 164–185.

Tatum, B. D. (1992). Talking about race, learning about racism: The application of racial identity development theory in the classroom. *Harvard Educational Review, 62*(1), 1–25.

Tatum, B. D. (1997). *Why are all the black kids sitting together in the cafeteria? A psychologist explains the development of racial identity* (5th ed.). New York: Basic Books.

Tatum, B. D. (2007). *Can we talk about race? And other conversations in an era of school resegregatio*n. Boston: Beacon Press.

Townsend, B. L. (2000). The disproportionate discipline of African American learners: Reducing school suspensions and expulsions. *Exceptional Children, 66*(3), 381–391.

Villegas, A. M., & Lucas, T. (2002). Preparing culturally responsive teachers: Reshaping the curriculum. *Journal of Teacher Education, 53*(1), 20–32.

Ware, F. (2006). Warm demander pedagogy: Culturally responsive teaching that supports a culture of achievement for African American students. *Urban Education, 41*(4), 427–456.

Warren, C. A. (2015). Conflicts and contradictions: Conceptions of empathy and the work of good-intentioned early career white female teachers. *Urban Education, 50*(5), 572–600.

Warren, C. A. (2018). Empathy, teacher dispositions, and preparation for culturally responsive pedagogy. *Journal of Teacher Education, 69*(2), 169–183.

Watkins, W. (2001). *The white architects of black education: Ideology and power in America.* New York: Teachers College Press.

Watson, H. L. (2012). The man with the dirty black beard: Race, class, and schools in the antebellum south. *Journal of the Early Republic, 32*(1), 1–26.

Webb, S. L. (2019). Everyday colorism: Reading in the language arts classroom. *English Journal, 108*(4), 21–28.

Weinstein, C. S., Curran, M., & Tomlinson-Clarke, S. (2003). Culturally responsive classroom management: Awareness into action. *Theory into Practice, 42*(4), 269–276.

Weissglass, J. (2001, August 8). Racism and the achievement gap. [Commentary]. *Education Week*, 49, 72.

Yosso, T. J. (2005). Whose culture has capital? A critical race theory discussion of community cultural wealth. *Race Ethnicity and Education, 8*(1), 69–91.

Index

The letter *f* following a page number denotes a figure.
Exercises are in all caps, homework handouts are indicated as such.

About the Author

Vernita Mayfield, PhD, hails originally from Los Angeles, California, where she began her career teaching elementary school. As a teacher, Mayfield found her first love serving and supporting students who have been historically marginalized. Since then, she has continued to do so through numerous positions of service including secondary school principal, researcher and lecturer, and educational consultant at state and national levels. In 2012, she founded Leadervation Learning to support organizations seeking to build leadership capacity, particularly in marginalized communities. The company evolved into a vehicle supporting leaders at all levels to understand and dismantle inequitable systems and organizations by building the cultural competency of staff.

Mayfield and her team deliver customized course development, comprehensive professional development, and consulting in cultural competency and racial healing. She is an inspiring speaker and the published author of numerous articles. This is her first book.

She holds a PhD in educational leadership and innovation and an EdS in educational administration from the University of Colorado, Denver. She earned an MBA from California State University, San Bernardino.